brand
FAILURES

Praise for *Brand Failures...*

"You learn more from failure than you can from success. Matt Haig's new book is a goldmine of helpful how-not-to advice, which you ignore at your own peril."

Laura Ries, President, Ries & Ries, marketing strategists, and bestselling co-author of *The Fall of Advertising and the Rise of PR* and *The 22 Immutable Laws of Branding*

"Every marketer will read this with both pleasure and profit. But the lessons are deadly serious, back to basics: real consumer benefits, value, execution. Read it, enjoy it, learn from it."

Patrick Barwise, Professor of Management and Marketing, London Business School

"Business books that manage to grab your attention, entertain you, and provide you with great advice, all at the same time, should be read immediately. This is one of those books. If you want to avoid being in the next edition of this book, you had better read it."

Peter Cheverton, CEO, Insight Marketing & People, and author of *Key Marketing Skills*

"I thought the book was terrific. Brings together the business lessons from all the infamous brand disasters from the Ford Edsel and New Coke to today's Andersen and Enron. A must-buy for marketers."

Peter Doyle, Professor of Marketing & Strategic Management, Warwick Business School, University of Warwick

"Brand Failures *is a treasure trove of information and insights. I'll be consulting it regularly!"*

Sicco van Gelder, CEO, Brand-Meta consultancy, and author of *Global Brand Strategy*

"Matt Haig is to be congratulated on compiling a comprehensive and compelling collection of 100 cases of failures attributable to misunderstanding or misapplication of brand strategy. Mark and learn."

Michael J Taylor, Emeritus Professor of Marketing, University of Strathclyde, President, Academy of Marketing

"The history of consumer marketing is littered with failed brands and we can learn from them. If you are responsible for your brand read this book. It might just be the best investment that you will ever make!"

Shaun Smith, Senior Vice President of Forum, a division of FT Knowledge, and author of *Uncommon Practice*

"Books that describe best branding practice abound and yet the real learning lies in studying why brands have failed. Matt Haig has done a terrific job in analysing this topic, and I highly recommend his book to everyone responsible for brand creation, development and management."

Dr Paul Temporal, Brand Strategy Consultant, Singapore (www.brandingasia.com) and author of *Advanced Brand Management*

brand
FAILURES

THE TRUTH ABOUT THE 100 BIGGEST
BRANDING MISTAKES OF ALL TIME

matt haig

**KOGAN
PAGE**

London and Sterling, VA

First published in Great Britain and the United States in 2003 by Kogan Page Limited

120 Pentonville Road
London N1 9JN
UK
www.kogan-page.co.uk

22883 Quicksilver Drive
Sterling VA 20166-2012
USA

ISBN 0 7494 3927 0

British Library Cataloguing-in-Publication Data

A CIP record for this book is available from the British Library.

Library of Congress Cataloging-in-Publication Data

Haig, Matt.
     Brand failures / Matt Haig.
          p. cm.
Includes bibliographical references and index.
     ISBN 0-7494-3927-0
     1. Brand name products--Marketing. 2. Brand loyalty. 3. Brand choice. I. Title
     HD69.B7H345 2003
     658.8'27--dc21

                                                                                    2003000966

Typeset by JS Typesetting Ltd, Wellingborough, Northants
Printed and bound in Great Britain by Biddles Ltd, Guildford and King's Lynn
www.biddles.co.uk

Contents

CHAPTER 1

Introduction

The process of branding was developed to protect products from failure. This is easy to see if we trace this process back to its 19th-century origins. In the 1880s, companies such as Campbell's, Heinz and Quaker Oats were growing ever more concerned about the consumer's reaction to mass-produced products. Brand identities were designed not only to help these products stand out, but also to reassure a public anxious about the whole concept of factory-produced goods.

By adding a 'human' element to the product, branding put the 19th-century shoppers' minds at rest. They may have once placed their trust in their friendly shopkeeper, but now they could place it in the brands themselves, and the smiling faces of Uncle Ben or Aunt Jemima which beamed down from the shop shelves.

The failure of mass-produced items that the factory owners had dreaded never happened. The brands had saved the day.

Fast-forward to the 21st century and a different picture emerges. Now it is the brands themselves that are in trouble. They have become a victim of their own success. If a product fails, it's the brand that's at fault.

They may have helped companies such as McDonald's, Nike, Coca-Cola and Microsoft build global empires, but brands have also transformed the process of marketing into one of perception-building. That is to say, image is now everything. Consumers make buying decisions based around the perception of the brand rather than the reality of the product. While this means brands can become more valuable than their physical assets, it also means they can lose this value overnight. After all, perception is a fragile thing.

If the brand image becomes tarnished through a media scandal or controversial incident or even a rumour spread via the Internet, then the company as a whole can find itself in deep trouble. Yet companies cannot opt out of this situation. They cannot turn the clock back to an age when branding didn't matter. And besides, they can grow faster than ever before through the creation of a strong brand identity.

So branding is no longer simply a way of averting failure. It is everything. Companies live or die on the strength of their brand.

Yet despite the fact that branding is more important than at any previous time, companies are still getting it wrong. In fact, they are worse at it than ever before. Brands are failing every single day and the company executives are left scratching their heads in bafflement.

The purpose of this book is to look at a wide variety of these brand failures, and brands which have so far managed to narrowly escape death, in order to explore the various ways in which companies can get it wrong.

As the examples show, brand failure is not the preserve of one certain type of business. Global giants such as Coca-Cola and McDonald's have proved just as likely to create brand flops as smaller and younger companies with little marketing experience.

It will also become clear that companies do not learn from each other's mistakes. In fact, the opposite seems to happen. Failure is an epidemic. It is contagious. Brands watch each other and replicate their mistakes. For instance, when the themed restaurant Planet Hollywood was still struggling to make a profit, a group of supermodels thought they should follow the formula with their own Fashion Café.

Companies are starting to suffer from 'lemming syndrome'. They are so busy following the competition that they don't realize when they are heading towards the cliff-edge. They see rival companies apply their brand name to new products, so they decide to do the same. They see others dive into new untested markets, so they do too.

While Coca-Cola and McDonald's may be able to afford the odd costly branding mistake, smaller companies cannot. For them, failure can be fatal. The branding process which was once designed to protect products is now itself filled with danger. While this danger can never be completely eliminated, by learning from the bad examples of others it is at least possible to identify where the main threats lie.

Why brands fail

A long, long time ago in a galaxy far away, products were responsible for the fate of a company. When a company noticed that its sales were flagging, it would come to one conclusion: its product was starting to fail. Now things have changed. Companies don't blame the product, they blame the *brand*.

It isn't the physical item sitting on the shop shelf at fault, but rather what that item represents, what it conjures up in the buyer's mind. This shift in thinking, from product-blame to brand-blame, is therefore related to the way buyer behaviour has changed.

'Today most products are bought, not sold,' write Al and Laura Ries in *The 22 Immutable Laws of Branding*. 'Branding "presells" the product or service to the user. Branding is simply a more efficient way to sell things.' Although this is true, this new focus means that perfectly good products can fail as a result of bad branding. So while branding raises the rewards, it also heightens the risks.

Scott Bedbury, Starbucks' former vice-president of marketing, controversially admitted that 'consumers don't truly believe there's a huge difference between products,' which means brands have to establish 'emotional ties' with their customers.

However, emotions aren't to be messed with. Once a brand has created that necessary bond, it has to handle it with care. One step out of line and the customer may not be willing to forgive.

This is ultimately why all brands fail. Something happens to break the bond between the customer and the brand. This is not always the fault of the company, as some things really are beyond their immediate control (global recession, technological advances, international disasters etc). However, more often than not, when brands struggle or fail it is usually down to a distorted perception of either the brand, the competition or the market. This altered view is a result of one of the following seven deadly sins of branding:

- *Brand amnesia*. For old brands, as for old people, memory becomes an increasing issue. When a brand forgets what it is supposed to stand for, it runs into trouble. The most obvious case of brand amnesia occurs when a venerable, long-standing brand tries to create a radical new identity, such as when Coca-Cola tried to replace its original formula with New Coke. The results were disastrous.
- *Brand ego*. Brands sometimes develop a tendency for over-estimating their own importance, and their own capability. This is evident when a brand believes it can support a market single-handedly, as Polaroid did with the instant photography market. It is also apparent when a brand enters a new

market for which it is clearly ill-suited, such as Harley Davidson trying to sell perfume.

- *Brand megalomania*. Egotism can lead to megalomania. When this happens, brands want to take over the world by expanding into every product category imaginable. Some, such as Virgin, get away with it. Most lesser brands, however, do not.

- *Brand deception*. 'Human kind cannot bear very much reality,' wrote T S Eliot. Neither can brands. Indeed, some brands see the whole marketing process as an act of covering up the reality of their product. In extreme cases, the trend towards brand fiction can lead to downright lies. For example, in an attempt to promote the film *A Knight's Tale* one Sony marketing executive invented a critic, and a suitable quote, to put onto the promotional poster. In an age where markets are increasingly connected, via the Internet and other technologies, consumers can no longer be deceived.

- *Brand fatigue*. Some companies get bored with their own brands. You can see this happening to products which have been on the shelves for many years, collecting dust. When brand fatigue sets in creativity suffers, and so do sales.

- *Brand paranoia*. This is the opposite of brand ego and is most likely to occur when a brand faces increased competition. Typical symptoms include: a tendency to file lawsuits against rival companies, a willingness to reinvent the brand every six months, and a longing to imitate competitors.

- *Brand irrelevance*. When a market radically evolves, the brands associated with it risk becoming irrelevant and obsolete. Brand managers must strive to maintain relevance by staying ahead of the category, as Kodak is trying to do with digital photography.

Brand myths

When their brands fail companies are always taken by surprise. This is because they have had faith in their brand from the start, otherwise it would never have been launched in the first place. However, this brand faith often stems from an obscured attitude towards branding, based around one or a combination of the following brand myths:

- *If a product is good, it will succeed.* This is blatantly untrue. In fact, good products are as likely to fail as bad products. Betamax, for instance, had better picture and audio quality than VHS video recorders. But it failed disastrously.
- *Brands are more likely to succeed than fail.* Wrong. Brands fail every single day. According to some estimates, 80 per cent of all new products fail upon introduction, and a further 10 per cent die within five years. By launching a product you are taking a one in ten chance of long-term success. As Robert McMath, a former Procter & Gamble marketing executive, once put it: 'it's easier for a product to fail than it is to survive.'
- *Big companies will always have brand success.* This myth can be dismantled with two words: New Coke. As this book will show, big companies have managed to have at least as much failure as success. No company is big enough to be immune to brand disaster. In fact, many of the examples in this book highlight one of the main paradoxes of branding – namely, that as brands get bigger and more successful, they also become more vulnerable and exposed.
- *Strong brands are built on advertising.* Advertising can support brands, but it can't build them from scratch. Many of the world's biggest brand failures accompanied extremely expensive advertising campaigns.
- *If it's something new, it's going to sell.* There may be a gap in the market, but it doesn't mean it has to be filled. This lesson was learnt the hard way for RJR Nabisco Holdings when they decided to launch a 'smokeless' cigarette. 'It took them a while to figure out that smokers actually like the smoke part of smoking,' one commentator said at the time.
- *Strong brands protect products.* This may have once been the case, but now the situation is reversed. Strong products now help to protect brands. As the cases show, the product has become the ambassador of the brand and even the slightest decrease in quality or a hint of trouble will affect the brand identity as a whole. The consumer can cause the most elaborate brand strategy to end in failure.

Why focus on failure?

The aim of this book is to provide 'how not to' advice by drawing on some of the largest branding blunders of all time. Brands which set sail with the help of multi-million dollar advertising campaigns shortly before sinking without trace are clear contenders. However, the book will also look at acknowledged brand mistakes made by usually successful companies such as Virgin, McDonald's, IBM, Coca-Cola, General Motors and many others.

Welcome, then, to the brand graveyard where companies have either put their flagging brand to rest or have allowed it to stagger around with no direction in a state of limbo. While these branding 'horror stories' may suggest that failure is inevitable, their example has helped to identify the key danger areas. It is hoped then, that this book will provide an illuminating, if rather frightening read.

Don't have nightmares.

CHAPTER 2

Classic failures

Some brand failures have proved so illuminating they have been discussed and dissected by marketing experts since they first happened. These 'classic' failures help to illustrate the fact that a product does not have to be particularly bad in order to flop.

Indeed, in the case of New Coke, the first failure we'll cover, the product was actually an enhancement of the formula it replaced. The reason it bombed was down to branding alone. Coca-Cola had forgotten what its core brand was meant to stand for. It naively thought that taste was the only factor consumers cared about. It was wrong.

In fact, all the examples in this chapter highlight fundamental marketing errors which many other brands have replicated since. These errors include such basic mistakes as setting the wrong price, choosing the wrong name, and getting too paranoid about the competition.

However, these failures also illustrate the general unpredictability of all marketing practices. No matter how strong a brand becomes, the market always remains elusive. The best any brand manager can hope for is to look out for any likely pitfalls which could catch them out. It is in the interest of identifying these pitfalls, rather than for the sake of *schadenfreude*, that the following classic failures are explored in some depth.

1 New Coke

Think of a brand success story, and you may well think of Coca-Cola. Indeed, with nearly 1 billion Coca-Cola drinks sold every single day, it is the world's most recognized brand.

Yet in 1985 the Coca-Cola Company decided to terminate its most popular soft drink and replace it with a formula it would market as New Coke. To understand why this potentially disastrous decision was made, it is necessary to appreciate what was happening in the soft drinks marketplace. In particular, we must take a closer look at the growing competition between Coca-Cola and Pepsi-Cola in the years and even decades prior to the launch of New Coke.

The relationship between the arch-rivals had not been a healthy one. Although marketing experts have believed for a long time that the competition between the two companies had made consumers more cola-conscious, the firms themselves rarely saw it like that. Indeed, the Coca-Cola company had even fought Pepsi-Cola in a legal battle over the use of the word 'cola' in its name, and lost.

Outside the courts though, Coca-Cola had always been ahead. Shortly after World War II, *Time* magazine was already celebrating Coke's 'peaceful near-conquest of the world.' In the late 1950s, Coke outsold Pepsi by a ratio of more than five to one. However, during the next decade Pepsi repositioned itself as a youth brand.

This strategy was a risky one as it meant sacrificing its older customers to Coca-Cola, but ultimately it proved successful. By narrowing its focus, Pepsi was able to position its brand against the old and classic image of its competitor. As it became increasingly seen as 'the drink of youth' Pepsi managed to narrow the gap.

In the 1970s, Coke's chief rival raised the stakes even further by introducing the Pepsi Challenge – testing consumers blind on the difference between its own brand and 'the real thing'. To the horror of Coca-Cola's long-standing company president, Robert Woodruff, most of those who participated preferred Pepsi's sweeter formula.

In the 1980s Pepsi continued its offensive, taking the Pepsi Challenge around the globe and heralding the arrival of the 'Pepsi Generation'. It also signed up celebrities likely to appeal to its target market such as Don Johnson and Michael Jackson (this tactic has survived into the new millennium, with figures like Britney Spears and Robbie Williams providing more recent endorsements).

By the time Roberto Goizueta became chairman in 1981, Coke's number one status was starting to look vulnerable. It was losing market share not only to Pepsi but also to some of the drinks produced by the Coca-Cola company itself, such as Fanta and Sprite. In particular the runaway success of Diet Coke was a double-edged sword, as it helped to shrink the sugar cola market. In 1983, the year Diet Coke moved into the number three position behind standard Coke and Pepsi, Coke's market share had slipped to an all-time low of just under 24 per cent.

Something clearly had to be done to secure Coke's supremacy. Goizueta's first response to the 'Pepsi Challenge' phenomenon was to launch an advertising campaign in 1984, praising Coke for being less sweet than Pepsi. The television ads were fronted by Bill Cosby, at that time one of the most familiar faces on the planet, and clearly someone who was too old to be part of the Pepsi Generation.

The impact of such efforts to set Coca-Cola apart from its rival was limited. Coke's share of the market remained the same while Pepsi was catching up. Another worry was that when shoppers had the choice, such as in their local supermarket, they tended to plump for Pepsi. It was only Coke's more effective distribution which kept it ahead. For instance, there were still considerably more vending machines selling Coke than Pepsi.

Even so, there was no getting away from the fact that despite the proliferation of soft drink brands, Pepsi was winning new customers. Having already lost on taste, the last thing Coca-Cola could afford was to lose its number one status.

The problem, as Coca-Cola perceived it, came down to the product itself. As the Pepsi Challenge had highlighted millions of times over, Coke could always be defeated when it came down to taste. This seemed to be confirmed by the success of Diet Coke which was closer to Pepsi in terms of flavour.

So in what must have been seen as a logical step, Coca-Cola started working on a new formula. A year later they had arrived at New Coke. Having produced its new formula, the Atlanta-based company conducted 200,000 taste tests to see how it fared. The results were overwhelming. Not only did it taste better than the original, but people preferred it to Pepsi-Cola as well.

However, if Coca-Cola was to stay ahead of Pepsi-Cola it couldn't have two directly competing products on the shelves at the same time. It therefore decided to scrap the original Coca-Cola and introduced New Coke in its place.

The trouble was that the Coca-Cola company had severely underestimated the power of its first brand. As soon as the decision was announced, a large percentage of the US population immediately decided to boycott the new product. On 23 April 1985 New Coke was introduced and a few days later the production of original Coke was stopped. This joint decision has since been referred to as 'the biggest marketing blunder of all time'. Sales of New Coke were low and public outrage was high at the fact that the original was no longer available.

It soon became clear that Coca-Cola had little choice but to bring back its original brand and formula. 'We have heard you,' said Goizueta at a press conference on 11 July 1985. He then left it to the company's chief operating officer Donald Keough to announce the return of the product.

Keough admitted:

> The simple fact is that all the time and money and skill poured into consumer research on the new Coca-Cola could not measure or reveal the deep and abiding emotional attachment to original Coca-Cola felt by so many people. The passion for original Coca-Cola – and that is the word for it, passion – was something that caught us by surprise. It is a wonderful American mystery, a lovely American enigma, and you cannot measure it any more than you can measure love, pride or patriotism.

In other words, Coca-Cola had learnt that marketing is about much more than the product itself. The majority of the tests had been carried out blind, and therefore taste was the only factor under assessment. The company had finally taken Pepsi's bait and, in doing so, conceded its key brand asset: originality.

When Coca-Cola was launched in the 1880s it was the only product in the market. As such, it invented a new category and the brand name became the name of the product itself. Throughout most of the last century, Coca-Cola capitalized on its 'original' status in various advertising campaigns. In 1942, magazine adverts appeared across the United States declaring: 'The only thing like Coca-Cola is Coca-Cola itself. It's the real thing.'

By launching New Coke, Coca-Cola was therefore contradicting its previous marketing efforts. Its central product hadn't been called new since the very first advert appeared in the *Atlanta Journal* in 1886, billing Coca-Cola as 'The New Pop Soda Fountain Drink, containing the properties of the wonderful Coca-plant and the famous Cola nuts.'

In 1985, a century after the product launched, the last word people associated with Coca-Cola was 'new'. This was the company with more allusions to US heritage than any other. Fifty years previously, the Pulitzer Prize winning editor of a Kansas newspaper, William Allen White had referred to the soft drink as the 'sublimated essence of all America stands for – a decent thing, honestly made, universally distributed, conscientiously improved with the years.' Coca-Cola had even been involved with the history of US space travel, famously greeting Apollo astronauts with a sign reading 'Welcome back to earth, home of Coca-Cola.'

To confine the brand's significance to a question of taste was therefore completely misguided. As with many big brands, the representation was more significant than the thing represented, and if any soft drink represented 'new' it was Pepsi, not Coca-Cola (even though Pepsi is a mere decade younger).

If you tell the world you have the 'real thing' you cannot then come up with a 'new real thing'. To borrow the comparison of marketing guru Al Ries it's 'like introducing a New God'. This contradictory marketing message was accentuated by the fact that, since 1982, Coke's strap line had been 'Coke is it'. Now it was telling consumers that they had got it wrong, as if they had discovered Coke *wasn't* it, but rather New Coke was instead.

So despite the tremendous amount of hype which surrounded the launch of New Coke (one estimate puts the value of New Coke's free publicity at over US $10 million), it was destined to fail. Although Coca-Cola's market researchers knew enough about branding to understand that consumers would go with their brand preference if the taste tests weren't blind, they failed to make the connection that these brand preferences would still exist once the product was launched.

Pepsi was, perhaps unsurprisingly, the first to recognize Coca-Cola's mistake. Within weeks of the launch, it ran a TV ad with an old man sitting on a park bench, staring at the can in his hand. 'They changed my Coke,' he said, clearly distressed. 'I can't believe it.'

However, when Coca-Cola relaunched its original coke, redubbed 'Classic Coke' for the US market, the media interest swung back in the brand's favour. It was considered a significant enough event to warrant a newsflash on ABC News and other US networks. Within months Coke had returned to the number one spot and New Coke had all but faded away.

Ironically, through the brand failure of New Coke loyalty to 'the real thing' intensified. In fact, certain conspiracy theorists have even gone so far as to say the whole thing had been planned as a deliberate marketing ploy to reaffirm public affection for Coca-Cola. After all, what better way to make someone appreciate the value of your global brand than to withdraw it completely?

Of course, Coca-Cola has denied that this was the company's intention. 'Some critics will say Coca-Cola made a marketing mistake, some cynics will say that we planned the whole thing,' said Donald Keough at the time. 'The truth is we are not that dumb, and we are not that smart.' But viewed in the context of its competition with Pepsi, the decision to launch New Coke was understandable. For years, Pepsi's key weapon had been the taste of its product. By launching New Coke, the Coca-Cola company clearly hoped to weaken its main rival's marketing offensive.

So what was Pepsi's verdict on the whole episode? In his book, *The Other Guy Blinked*, Pepsi's CEO Roger Enrico believes the error of New Coke proved to be a valuable lesson for Coca-Cola. 'I think, by the end of their nightmare, they figured out who they really are. Caretakers. They can't change the taste of their flagship brand. They can't change its imagery. All they can do is defend the heritage they nearly abandoned in 1985.'

Lessons from New Coke

- *Concentrate on the brand's perception.* In the words of Jack Trout, author of *Differentiate or Die*, 'marketing is a battle of perceptions, not products'.
- *Don't clone your rivals.* In creating New Coke, Coca-Cola was reversing its brand image to overlap with that of Pepsi. The company has made similar mistakes both before and after, launching Mr Pibb to rival Dr Pepper and Fruitopia to compete with Snapple.
- *Feel the love.* According to Saatchi and Saatchi's worldwide chief executive officer, Kevin Roberts, successful brands don't have 'trademarks'. They have 'lovemarks' instead. In building brand loyalty, companies are also creating an emotional attachment that often has little to do with the quality of the product.
- *Don't be scared to U-turn.* By going back on its decision to scrap original Coke, the company ended up creating an even stronger bond between the product and the consumer.
- *Do the right market research.* Despite the thousands of taste tests Coca-Cola carried out on its new formula, it failed to conduct adequate research into the public perception of the original brand.

2 The Ford Edsel

Among many US marketing professors, the story of the Edsel car is considered the classic brand failure of all time. Dubbed 'the Titanic of automobiles', the Edsel is certainly one of the biggest branding disasters to afflict the Ford Motor Company.

As with other, more recent brand failures featured in the book (see New Coke, WAP and boo.com for three examples), the Edsel car was launched amid a vast amount of hype. Although the car didn't appear in showrooms until September 1957, ads promoting it had begun to appear months previously bearing the teaser slogan: 'The Edsel is Coming'.

Ford decided though, to fuel public interest, the car itself should not be seen in the ads, and even when Ford dealers started stocking the car in their showrooms, they were told they had to keep the vehicles undercover. If they did not they risked a fine and the loss of their franchise with the company.

As Ford hoped, interest was fuelled. The company did not think for one moment that the product would not be able to match the hype, and would lead to a consumer backlash. After all, more work and research had gone into the development of this car than almost any previously.

However, some of the research had already proven futile by the time of the launch. For instance, part of the market research process had been to find a suitable name for the new car. This should have been a good idea. After all, the highly popular Ford Thunderbird car, which had been launched in 1954, had gained its evocative name as a result of market research findings. This time, research teams were sent out to New York, Chicago and Michigan, where members of the public were asked what they thought of certain names and to come up with their own suggestions. There was also a competition among employees to come up with the best name, and the company even contacted the popular poet Marianne Moore. Her brief was to find a name which would signify a 'visceral feeling of elegance, fleetness, advanced features and design.' Her rather eccentric suggestions included Mongoose Civique, Resilient Bullet, Utopian Turtletop and the Varsity Stroke.

Altogether, the company now had a pool of 10,000 names to choose from. Too many, according to company chairman, Ernest Breech, as he scanned through the names during a meeting of the Ford Executive Committee in November 1956. 'Why don't we just call it Edsel?' he asked, exasperated. Henry Ford II, the grandson of Henry Ford, agreed. Edsel was the name of his father, and the Ford founder's only son.

Not everyone held the same opinion though. The PR director, C Gayle Warnock, knew that Edsel was not the right name. It had been an early suggestion, and had not been liked by those members of the public who had taken part in the market research (in word-association tests, it had been associated with 'weasel' and 'pretzel' – hardly the best associations for a dynamic new car). Warnock had preferred other names on the list, such as Pacer, Ranger, Corsair or Citation. When the decision was made, Warnock made his feelings perfectly clear. According to Robert Lacey in his book *Ford: The Men and the Machine*, Warnock responded to the new Edsel name by declaring: 'We have just lost 200,000 sales.' For Warnock, a rose by any other name clearly didn't smell as sweet.

As it turned out, the name was the least of the Edsel's problems. There was also the design.

The first blueprint for the Edsel looked truly impressive, as Robert Lacey writes in his book on Ford. 'With concealed airscoops below the bumpers, this first version of the car was original and dramatic – a dreamlike, ethereal creation which struck those who saw it as the very embodiment of the future.' However, this magnificent design never got to see the light of day. The people who held onto the purse strings at Ford decided it would simply be too expensive to manufacture.

The design that eventually emerged was certainly unique. Edsel's chief designer, Roy Brown Jr had always set out to design a car that would be recognizable instantly, from any direction. And indeed, there is no denying that the first Edsels to emerge in 1957 fulfilled this objective. In particular, the car's front-end bonnet and grille commanded the most attention. 'The front end design was the most prominent feature,' confirms Phil Skinner, a respected Edsel historian, 'If you consider other cars from the mid-1950s, they all looked somewhat alike. Basically it was two headlights and a horizontal grille. By having the big impact ring in the middle – what we now call a horse collar – it really set the Edsel apart.'

Although some members of the automotive press commended this distinctive look, most were unappreciative. One reviewer famously remarked that it looked 'like an Oldsmobile sucking a lemon.' While another thought the front-end grille was less like a horse collar, and more like a toilet seat. (The customer comments later proved to be even worse with some saying that the grille looked like a 'vagina with teeth'.

However, Ford had good relations with the press and Warnock, the PR director, was determined to maximize the media coverage immediately before and after the launch date. Articles subsequently appeared in both *Time* and *Life* magazines heralding the Edsel as a breakthrough and explaining how it had been planned for over a decade – a blatant exaggeration on the part of Warnock as Roy Brown had only begun designing the car in 1954. The promotional brochure to mark the September launch of the Edsel also promised a great deal. 'There has never been a car like the Edsel,' it promised. This was a big claim, but Ford had equally big ambitions. The company expected to produce 200,000 units in the car's first year. This constituted around five per cent of the entire market.

Anyway, the pre-publicity had initially seemed to work. Car showrooms became packed with curious visitors, desperately seeking their first glance of the car. In the first week of its launch, almost three million members of the US public visited Edsel showrooms. The Edsels they saw had a number of distinct features, in addition to the 'love-it-or-hate-it' front-end grille. For instance, the car was the first ever to have self-adjusting brakes and an electronic hood release. It also had a very powerful engine for a medium-range car. However, these features weren't enough.

In the minds of the public, the car simply didn't live up to the hype. And unfortunately for Ford, neither did the sales. Edsel sold only 64,000 units in its first year, way below the number anticipated. Ford launched 1959 and 1960 Edsel models but sales fell even further (to 44,891 and 2,846 respectively). In November 1959 Ford printed the last ever ad for the car and halted production.

So what had gone wrong? In the case of Edsel there are almost too many reasons to identify. In fact, it would be easier to ask: what *hadn't* gone wrong?

The marketing campaign was certainly a key factor. In simple terms, Ford had overstated its case. Buoyed by the success of the Thunderbird only a few years previously the company must have felt invincible, and this was reflected in the rather too self-assured advertising material.

However, no-one can excuse Ford of underexposure. On 13 October 1957 the marketing campaign for Edsel took product promotion to new heights when Ford joined forces with the CBS television network, to run a one-hour special called *The Edsel Show*. The show, a parody of 1950s favourite *The Ed Sullivan Show* featured celebrities such as Frank Sinatra and Bing Crosby. But even with such prime-time promotion Ford was unable to shift anywhere near enough units of the car. Consumers didn't care whether it was 'revolutionary' or not. All they knew was that it looked ugly and had a name that sounded like 'weasel'. Furthermore, in an age when all the successful cars had tailfins, the Edsel was finless. According to Bob Casey, curator of transportation at the Henry Ford Museum, this fact meant that the Edsel 'didn't quite fit into people's vision of a car'.

In addition to misguided advertising, bad looks and a stupid name, Edsel faced a further problem – it was too expensive. As Sheila Mello explains in her informative book, *Customer Centric Product Definition*, the launch of the Edsel coincided with a move towards cheaper models:

> Ford's decision to highlight the Edsel's powerful engine during a period when the buying public was gravitating toward smaller, more fuel-efficient cars alienated potential customers. The first models in the showroom were the most expensive, top-of-the-line models, resulting in what we refer to today as sticker shock. Unfortunately, too, while some Edsel models were more expensive than comparable cars, they had an equivalent or greater number of quality problems. Often parts did not fit properly or were simply missing, since Ford frequently built Edsels between Fords and Mercurys on the same assembly line. Many dealers were ill equipped to replace these parts or add accessories.

The car ended up looking more expensive than it actually was because of poor timing. In the 1950s, US new car models typically appeared in November for the following year. For instance, a 1956 Thunderbird would have come out in November 1955. However, Edsel was launched in September, two months before the other new models arrived. It was therefore a 1958 car competing against 1957 models – and more importantly, 1957 prices.

In fact, the situation was even worse than that. Not only had Edsel decided to push its most expensive models first, but the 1957 models it was competing with were being offered at a discounted price in order to sell them before next year's models were wheeled into the showroom.

A high price may have been acceptable if it had been worth paying. However, the experience of those few early Edsel customers quickly gave the car a reputation for mechanical problems. Edsel now popularly stood for Every Day Something Else Leaks.

One thing though was completely beyond Ford's control. After a boom period for the US car industry during the mid-1950s, the end of 1957 saw the start of a recession. In 1958 almost all car models saw a drop in sales, some by as much as 50 per cent. Ironically, one of the very few models to witness an increase in sales that year was the Ford Thunderbird.

In a September 1989 article for *The Freeman*, a publication of The Foundation for Economic Education, car industry journalist Anthony Young explained how Ford had paid little attention to market research, and that this was the true reason why the Edsel failed:

> The Edsel serves as a textbook example of corporate presumption and disregard for market realities. It also demonstrates that advertising and pre-delivery hype have their limits in inducing consumers to buy a new and unproven car. In a free market economy, it is the car-buying public, not the manufacturer, that determines the success or failure of an automobile. A manufacturer shouldn't oversell a new car, or unrealistic expectations will be built up in the minds of consumers. If the newly introduced car doesn't live up to expectations, it is practically doomed on the showroom floor.

However, Ford quickly learnt its lesson. A few years later the spectacular failure of the Edsel was counterbalanced by the equally spectacular success of the Ford Mustang. Launched in 1964, the Mustang sold half a million vehicles in its first year of production. Not only did it have a better name and a good-looking bonnet, the Mustang had one further advantage over its predecessor – it was affordable.

As Sheila Mello points out, between 1960 (when the Edsel was phased out) and 1964 (when the Mustang was launched) Ford, along with most of the car industry, had shifted its focus towards what the consumer actually wanted. 'The success of the Mustang demonstrates that Ford Motor Company did learn from the Edsel experience,' she writes. 'The key difference between the ill-fated development of the Edsel and the roaring success of the

Mustang was the shift from a product-centric focus to a customer-centric one.'

This view is supported by Lee Iacocca, who oversaw the creation of the Mustang as Ford president, before taking over the reins at Chrysler. In his autobiography, Iacocca explains the approach behind the Mustang: 'Whereas the Edsel had been a car in search of a market it never found, here was a market in search of a car. The normal procedure in Detroit was to build a car and then try to identify its buyers. But we were in a position to move in the opposite direction – and tailor a new product for a hungry new market.' As a result, the Mustang went from strength to strength and is still in production today.

So while the whole Edsel episode may have been a costly embarrassment for Ford in the short term, it helped the company learn some valuable lessons which it has carried with it to this day.

Lessons from Edsel

- *Hyping an untested product is a mistake.* 'I learned that a company should never allow its spokespersons to build up enthusiasm for an unseen, unproven product,' confessed C Gayle Warnock, the PR director responsible for the publicity surrounding the Edsel launch.
- *Your name matters.* At the most basic level, your brand *is* your name. It doesn't matter how important the brand name is to the company, it's what it means to the public that counts. If the name conjures up images of weasels and pretzels it might be a good time to scrap it.
- *Looks count.* Visual appearance is a key factor in creating a brand identity for most products. It was the distinctive shape of Coca-Cola bottles which helped that brand become so big. In the car industry, looks are particularly important and as Edsel proved, ugly ducklings don't always become swans.
- *Price is important.* Products can be too expensive or too cheap. When some brands price themselves too low, they lose their prestige. However, with a car such as the Edsel, the high price couldn't be justified in the minds of the public.
- *The right research is important.* Ford spent time and money carrying out the wrong kind of market research. Instead of hunting for names, the company should have been concentrating on whether there was a market for its new car in the first place. As it turned out, the market it spent millions trying to reach didn't even exist.

- *Quality is important.* Of course, product quality is always important but when it comes to cars it is a matter of life and death. Bad quality control proved an extra nail in Edsel's coffin.

3 Sony Betamax

According to received branding wisdom, the best way to become a strong brand is to be first in a new category. This theory has been repeatedly emphasized by the world-renowned brand guru Al Ries.

'Customers don't really care about new brands, they care about new categories,' he writes in *The 22 Immutable Laws of Branding*. 'By first pre-empting the category and then aggressively promoting the category, you create both a powerful brand and a rapidly escalating market.'

There are indeed a number of cases to support this point. Domino's was the first company to offer home-delivered pizza and remains the leader in that particular market. Coca-Cola, the world's most popular and financially successful brand, was the first in the cola category.

As Chapter 9 will make clear, this theory breaks down, however, in technology markets. Owing to the fact that consumer behaviour tends to be approximately five years behind technological breakthroughs, the first mover advantage is often lost. Furthermore, companies have often proved to be very bad at predicting how new technologies will be used. For example, most of the European mobile phone companies were caught completely unaware by the rapid rise of text messaging, a facility which some didn't even bother to explain in their instructions booklets.

The all-time classic among technology brand failures was Sony's Betamax video recorders. During the 1970s, Sony developed a machine designed to deliver home video-taping equipment. The machine used Betamax technology, and hit the stores in 1975. In its first year, 30,000 Betamax video recorders (or VCRs) were sold in the United States alone. But a year later Sony's rival JVC came out with the VHS – short for 'video home system' –

format VCR. By January 1977, there were four more Japanese electronics companies manufacturing and marketing VHS-based machines.

Whereas Sony had either been unwilling or unable to license Betamax technology (depending on which account you believe), JVC had been more than happy sharing their VHS format. This would later prove a critical factor in the demise of Betamax.

Although Sony pioneered most of the advancements, JVC and the other VHS manufacturers were not slow to catch up. For instance, JVC and Panasonic introduced VHS hi-fi formats only weeks after Sony's introduction of Betamax hi-fi. However, most experts agree that the tape quality on Betamax was superior to that of its rival.

As the two formats were incompatible, consumers were forced to decide between them. Pretty soon Sony was feeling under pressure as its competitors started to drop prices to as much as US $300 below Sony's machines. By 1982 the price war was in full swing and Sony reluctantly joined in, offering a US $50 rebate as a 'Home Improvement Grant'.

There were other marketing problems too. Up until the early 1980s the word 'Betamax' was used as a synonym for 'video recorder'. This association had negative as well as positive consequences because in 1979, Universal Studios and Disney took legal action against Sony, claiming VCRs were infringing the copyrights of movie producers. Although Sony emerged apparently unscathed from the lawsuit, several commentators have suggested that the case had a detrimental impact on the way Sony marketed its Betamax products.

One thing is for sure, from 1981 onwards Betamax-based machines were rapidly losing popular favour. In 1982, the year of the price war, Betamax VCRs accounted for a paltry 25 per cent of the entire market and the public were being warned that the selection of video rentals available for Betamax owners would be slightly smaller than that for VHS owners.

Furthermore, while Sony continued to claim that Betamax was a technically superior format, video owners were becoming increasingly aware of one serious failing. Whereas VHS machines could record for a considerable length of time, Betamax machines could only record for one hour – meaning that most films and football matches couldn't be recorded in one go. This was the price Sony paid for enhanced sound and picture quality. To deliver that better standard, Sony used a bigger, slower moving tape. As a result, it sometimes took as many as three cassettes to show an entire movie. This caused frustration both among video owners, who had to swap tapes over, and retailers, who had to supply more cassettes. The problem is explained by one anonymous VHS fan on the blockinfo.com Web site: 'What made VHS succeed was that you could get a whole movie on a tape. Okay, maybe the picture and sound weren't as good as Beta; but what the heck, you didn't have to get up in the middle and switch cassettes. VHS delivered value on a dimension that mattered to consumers. Beta delivered excellent value on dimensions that did not.' Sony refused to bite the bullet though. Indeed, it may have been losing market share but the number of units sold still continued to rise, peaking with global sales of 2.3 million units in 1984.

However, three years later VHS had gone way beyond the tipping point with a 95 per cent share of the market. In 1987, *Rolling Stone* magazine ran an article on Betamax (entitled 'Format Wars') and declared 'the battle is over'. On 10 January 1988 Sony finally swallowed its pride and announced plans for a VHS line of video recorders.

Although Sony was adamant that the press should not see this as the 'death' of Betamax, the press weren't listening. On 25 January, only a fortnight after Sony's announcement, *Time* magazine published a eulogy to the brand with the headline, 'Goodbye Beta'.

The same article also argued that Betamax had failed because it had refused to license the format to other firms. 'While at first Sony kept its Beta technology mostly to itself, JVC, the Japanese inventor of VHS, shared its secret with a raft of other firms.' This claim has since been hotly disputed by the defenders of Betamax. For instance, one AFU (Alt Folklore Urban) white paper on *The Decline and Fall of Betamax* refers to the statement as 'blatantly untrue'. According to James Lardner, author of *Fast Forward*, Sony invited JVC and Matsushita to license the Betamax technology in December 1974, but both companies declined the offer.

Either way, the fact that Betamax video recorders were only manufactured by Sony meant that it couldn't compete against the growing number of companies pushing VHS. However, even when Sony started to make VHS machines it didn't abandon Betamax. Overseas production of Betamax hobbled on until 1998, and in Sony's home territory, Japan, machines were still being made until 2002, although not in huge numbers (Sony produced just 2,800 units in 2001).

On 22 August 2002 Sony finally announced it would be discontinuing Betamax products. 'With digital machines and other new recording formats taking hold in the market, demand has continued to decline and it has become difficult to secure parts,' the company said in a statement.

Now, of course, VHS itself is under threat from the rapid rise in digital versatile disc (DVD) players, and may not be able to survive into the long term. While DVD has finally drawn a line under the battle between Betamax and VHS, it has also managed to create its own destructive war between different DVD formats, and therefore delayed the take-off of that market.

However, at least some of the lessons of Betamax have been learnt. Sony and eight of its competitors eventually joined forces in 2002 to create a common format for DVD, meaning this time Sony will not be left on the sidelines.

Lessons from Betamax

- *Don't go it alone.* 'Contrary to popular belief, what would help every category pioneer is competition,' says Al Ries. True, providing the competition isn't pushing a format incompatible with your own.
- *Let others in.* Whether Sony refused to license its format or not, there is no question that the company would have had a better chance if its rivals had adopted Betamax.
- *Cut your losses.* Sony's decision to ignore VHS until 1987 was, with hindsight, an undeniable mistake.
- *Supply equals demand.* When the manufacturers of pre-recorded tapes decreased their supply of Beta format tapes, demand for Sony's Betamax recorders inevitably waned.

4 McDonald's Arch Deluxe

As well as the McLibel Trial (covered in Chapter 5), McDonald's has also experienced a number of more conventional marketing problems in recent years. Most of these problems have been new products that have failed to inspire consumers. McLean Deluxe (an attempt to cater for the health-conscious customer) and McSoup are two obvious examples, but it was with the Arch Deluxe burger that McDonald's experienced its most embarrassing flop.

Marketed as the 'Burger with the Grown-up Taste', the idea was to have a burger which wasn't associated with children. Indeed, the advertising campaign for the Arch Deluxe rammed the message home with various images of kids shunning the 'sophisticated' product.

The trouble was that nobody goes to McDonald's for sophistication, they go for convenience. Part of this convenience is knowing exactly what to expect. McDonald's restaurants may serve up gazpacho in Spain and lamb burgers in India, but on the whole they are the same the world over. Most people who walk into a McDonald's restaurant know what they are going to order before they reach the counter. They don't want to be bombarded with a million and one variations on what is essentially the same product – a hamburger.

The other problem with the Arch Deluxe was the fact that it was sold on taste. Everybody knows that McDonald's is never going to be awarded a Michelin star, yet everybody still comes back. In an article headlined 'McDonald's Missing the Mark,' which appeared in *Brand Week* on 12

November 2001, Dave Miller attacked the 'compete on taste' strategy apparent in the promotion of the Arch Deluxe:

> We don't come to the Golden Arches on the merits of taste and tantalization and culinary delight. We prize your brand on friendliness, cleanliness, consistency and convenience. They are value propositions that you've abdicated in recent years and – luckily – competitors have neglected to capture. Exactly how many failed menu concepts does it take before all of those development dollars are instead ploughed into the value proposition?

However, the problems encountered with the Arch Deluxe are symptomatic of an even bigger problem. As with other brands of such an enormous scale, McDonald's has been accused of losing touch with its customers and being too far behind the market.

Indeed, this is a problem acknowledged by the company's CEO, Jack Greenberg, who arrived in 1998. 'We have been taking much too long to develop an idea and get it to the market, then too long to decide whether we want to do it or not,' he told *The Financial Times* in that same year (in an article entitled 'A mission to buff up the golden arches').

As you would expect with a brand that has built its name through uniformity, McDonald's is heavily centralized. Most branding and marketing decisions need to go through the company's headquarters in Oak Brook, Illinois. The recipe for the Arch Deluxe itself came from the Oak Brook kitchen. This contrasts with McDonald's major product successes such as the Big Mac, the Hot Apple Pie, the Egg McMuffin and the Filet o' Fish, which were all invented in operators' kitchens out in the field (whereas other flops such as the McLean burger and McPizza were also conjured up at the Oak Brook headquarters).

Another interesting aspect of the Arch Deluxe failure is that the product was well researched. After conducting masses of market research, it emerged that people would love to eat a burger designed specifically for adults. Unfortunately, these people seemed to be in short supply when the product was finally launched.

Lessons from Arch Deluxe

- *Go for what you know*. Part of McDonald's brand identity is simplicity. Another part is its child-friendly approach. A 'sophisticated' burger designed to exclude children was therefore destined to misfire.
- *Avoid customer confusion*. 'McDonald's is not cognitive, it is reflexive,' says Dave Miller in the November 2001 *Brand Week* article. 'We treasure not having to think about it. It just "is".' By extending its range with products such as the Arch Deluxe, Bratwursts, McTacos and McMussels, McDonald's was creating a need to think.
- *Be sceptical of research*. Market research has its place when carefully conducted, but it should never be taken as gospel truth.

CHAPTER 3

Idea failures

As the examples in this book illustrate, there are numerous reasons why brands fail. Sometimes it is because the market they are associated with has become obsolete. Other times it is as a result of extending into an unsuitable product category. In some, dramatic cases it is the result of a high-profile scandal which causes the public to boycott the brand.

Often though, the reason for failure is more straightforward. Many brands fail because they are simply bad ideas that haven't been properly researched. Occasionally these failures are the result of strong, established brands coming up with a new variation of their product. Understanding that new product categories should be avoided, brands stay within their original category but come up with a bizarre twist on the formula. But why should that matter? After all, branding isn't about products, it is about perception. This is the new marketing mantra. And yet, there is no escaping the fact that at least part of this perception centres around the product itself.

The cleverest brand strategy in the world cannot make consumers buy a product they don't want. Or at least, it can't make them buy it more than once. While it is true that the market leader is not always the best in terms of quality, it is equally true that if a product is truly bad or truly pointless it will be unable to find eager customers.

The real question is, how do bad products appear in the first place? If the consumer doesn't want them, why invent them? Because companies still insist that they know better than their customers. It is certainly true that market research has failings of its own. As Henry Ford remarked on the launch of his Model T, 'if I had asked the customer, he would have asked for a faster horse.'

The problem is that what companies consider sublime, the customer all too often treats as ridiculous. Bottled mineral water for dogs? Great idea, says the company. A joke, responds the customer.

Even some of the world's most successful brands have been guilty of introducing incredibly bad products. For instance, in 1995 Microsoft came up with the idea of a 'social interface' called Bob. The idea was that Bob, a helpful animated man with glasses (looking not dissimilar to Bill Gates), would provide help and information in a 'conversational, social style.' To add to Bob's personality, he was given a number of 'friends' such as Rover the dog, Scuzz the sewer rat and a 'friendly dragon'. The product was aimed at adults, yet no-one old enough to tie their own shoelaces wanted to use it.

Throughout this chapter similar failures are drawn upon in order to show that branding is futile if the consumer doesn't like the product.

5 Kellogg's Cereal Mates

Warm milk, frosty reception

Kellogg's may have had problems when marketing in certain foreign territories such as India (see Chapter 6), but the company has also come unstuck on its home turf, most notably with its Cereal Mates product.

The idea was simple. Cereal Mates were small boxes of Kellogg's cereal packed with a container of milk and a plastic spoon. The advantage of the product was equally straightforward. Namely, convenience. An increase in working hours in the United States, combined with the rise in fast-food chains, led Kellogg's to believe that there was a demand for an 'all-in-one' breakfast product. To maximize Cereal Mates' chances of success, the line included the four most powerful Kellogg's brands in the US – namely Corn Flakes, Frosted Flakes (Frosties), Fruit Loops, and Mini Wheats.

However, despite Kellogg's best efforts, the Cereal Mates brand proved a major flop, and in 1999, the year Kellogg's rival General Mills took over as the United States' number one cereal maker, the product was pulled from the shelves.

The reasons why Cereal Mates failed to win over consumers are various, and have been dissected by various journalists and marketing professionals. Here are some of the main factors behind Cereal Mates' brand failure:

- *Factor one: warm milk.* As each container of milk was 'aseptically packaged,' it didn't need refrigeration. However, consumers didn't like the idea of warm milk.

- *Factor two*: *cool milk*. In order to accommodate for the consumer's preference for cool milk, Kellogg's eventually decided to place Cereal Mates in refrigerators to imply that consumers should have the milk cold. However, as Robert McMath, president of New Product Works and author of *What Were They Thinking?*, has observed, this led to even more confusion. 'This decision inevitably caused a problem in that Cereal Mates was not in a location where you would generally expect to find breakfast cereal. The expense of trying to re-educate the consumer to look for cereal in the dairy case proved too enormous – way beyond, apparently, what Kellogg's wanted to spend on selling the new line,' writes McMath.
- *Factor three*: *advertising*. As if the consumer wasn't confused enough, Kellogg's complicated matters further with the advertising campaign for Cereal Mates. The TV ads featured young kids helping themselves to the product, while their parents lay snoring contentedly in bed. However, the packaging of the product was far from child-friendly, and if they left their kids to help themselves, the parents would have probably been crying (or at least getting cross) over spilt milk.
- *Factor four*: *the taste*. Even when picked up from a refrigerator, the product was often consumed at work or away from home. In other words, when the milk was warm and tasted terrible.
- *Factor five*: *the price*. Retailing at way over a dollar, Cereal Mates was considered too expensive by many consumers.

These factors, working in conjunction, caused the Cereal Mates brand to fail. And so, after two years on the shelves (or in refrigerators), Kellogg's pulled the plug on the product.

However, there may be one more reason why Cereal Mates failed to spark a revolution in breakfast habits. As a convenience food, it simply wasn't convenient enough. A February 2000 article in *Newsweek* ('Crunch time at Kellogg'), looked at the changing demands for breakfast products, and the consequences for the cereal company.

Americans' hectic new morning routine is wreaking havoc on Kellogg Co. Killer commutes (nearly an hour round trip in many cities) leave no time to fix even the simplest breakfast. Getting out the door is equally challenging for the 64 percent of families in which both parents work. More Americans than ever simply skip breakfast, according to new data from NPD Group, an eating-habits researcher. 'People wish they could just get breakfast injected into them on the run,' says Gerald Celente, editor of the *Trends Journal*, a marketing-industry newsletter.

Cereal Mates may have enabled people to take their cereal with them, but they still had to pour the milk over it, and spend valuable time eating the cereal with a small spoon. As Keith Naughton concluded in the article above, Breakfast Mates 'failed to catch on because it was impossible to eat while driving.'

Indeed, where Kellogg's has had success in the convenience food market it is with breakfast bars such as Nutri-grain. Unlike Cereal Mates, these bars can be consumed in seconds, and on the move. Moreover, they don't involve warm milk.

Lessons from Kellogg's Cereal Mates

- *Consumers don't like warm milk on their cereal.* OK, I think we've established that one.
- *Don't mix your messages.* On the one hand, Cereal Mates was an 'eat anywhere' product. On the other, Kellogg's was implying it needed to be stored in a refrigerator.
- *Sell the brand in the right place.* Cereal Mates was, essentially, a cereal rather than a milk product. Consumers would have therefore expected to see it on the shelves next to the other cereal products.
- *Be the best in at least one thing.* As a cereal product Cereal Mates failed because there were tastier and equally healthy alternatives. As a convenience product it failed because breakfast bars proved to be a faster, more flexible option.
- *Don't price too high.* Consumers did not expect to pay as much as they did for a four ounce box of cereal.

6 Sony's *Godzilla*

A monster flop

If one word saturates the brand consultant's vocabulary more than any other, it is 'synergy'. When big companies formulate a brand strategy they increasingly try to *synergize* their marketing efforts. In other words, the aim is to extend the brand into other relevant product categories.

In recent times, cross-promotional tie-ins have become all the rage and have proven, if indeed proof was needed, that brands have become larger than the specific products they represent. This trend is particularly obvious within the entertainment industry.

Take pop music. Gone are the days when all that mattered was what a pop group sounded like. Now, it is all about branding. As Michael J Wolf tells us in *The Entertainment Economy*, 'brands and stars have become the same thing'. Ever since the Spice Girls phenomenon, record executives have been spending as much time thinking of ways to strike deals with toy manufacturers, television executives and fast-food chains as they have about pushing singles and albums. In the case of a band like SClub7, the brand extensions were planned right from the start, with the SClub's debut single and TV show appearing simultaneously. TV series such as the UK's *Popstars* and the US series *American Idol*, where popstars are created through the show itself, also exemplify this new way to cross-publicize an entertainment brand via different media.

Nowhere, however, is brand synergy more apparent than in the world of movies. George Lucas' *Star Wars* franchise was the first to exploit the full possibilities of brand extension. As well as through movies, consumers have been able to interact with the *Star Wars* brand in numerous other ways. They have bought *Star Wars* action figures, read *Star Wars* novels, played the *Star Wars* computer game and worn *Star Wars* pyjamas.

Now of course, we are used to the 'movie as brand' concept. *Men in Black, The Lord of the Rings, Harry Potter, Toy Story, Monsters Inc.* and numerous others have replicated *Star Wars'* cross-branded success. While this means the Hollywood studios can make potentially more money than ever before from a movie, it also means they have more to lose if things don't go to plan. Just ask Sony.

With the 1998 release of *Godzilla*, Sony believed it had created a monster movie hit. Indeed, it is difficult to think of a movie that looked more likely to become a blockbuster. Sony had spent US $60 million implementing the teaser campaign. They had Puff Daddy rapping his way through one of the most expensive promo videos ever made for the *Godzilla* theme tune. Furthermore, a replica of the star of the movie – a skyscraper-high green monster – was guaranteed to make a fantastic toy.

Most significantly, owing to Sony's newly consolidated cinema holdings, the film was shown on more screens in its opening weekend than any other in movie history. On the day of its launch, one in five cinema screens were playing *Godzilla*.

The only trouble was that for all the money spent on a slick ad campaign, the word of mouth publicity surrounding the film was pretty bad. Even before the movie launched, news was spreading on the Internet of just how terrible it was. However, Sony was determined to get the online reviewers on side. The company even paid for Harry Knowles, the owner of the highly influential site AintItCoolNews, to fly out for the premiere in New York. But nothing could stop the growing number of terrible reviews. Here is an extract from James Berardinelli's one star review which appeared on the movie-reviews.net site on the day the film opened:

> Godzilla is the ultimate culmination of the 'who cares about plot' summer movie. A loose remake of the 1954 'classic' Japanese monster movie, Godzilla, King of the Monsters, Roland Emmerich and Dean Devlin's big-budget lizard-stomps-Manhattan disaster flick has been written with the brain dead in mind. The script isn't 'dumbed down', it's lobotomised. [. . .] Worst of all, Godzilla isn't even exciting. With

the possible exception of a mildly enjoyable car chase near the end, there isn't a sequence in this film that raises the pulse. Even the scenes with dozens of aircraft attacking the monster are so devoid of tension and suspense that they are yawn-provoking. Independence Day may have been dumb, but it was full of 'adrenaline moments' capable of getting the audience involved in the action. In this aspect of its production, as in so many others, Godzilla is lacking. Actually, part of the problem is that we're never sure who we're supposed to be rooting for: the green monster with an attitude or the paper-thin humans trying to stop him.

Towards the end of the review, Berardinelli emphasized the insignificance of his opinion:

Ultimately, it doesn't really matter what I (or any other critic, for that matter) have to say about the movie. Sony's TriStar has assumed that Godzilla, like all self-proclaimed summer event motion pictures, is pretty much critic-proof. It may also be word-of-mouth-proof. Those who want to see the movie will see it no matter what I write or their friends say. So, when I go on record to assert that Godzilla is one of the most idiotic blockbuster movies of all time, it's like spitting into the wind.

Maybe if Berardinelli's had been the only bad review he would have had a point. But when there were thousands of other everyday moviegoers – not high-minded newspaper critics – venting their negative opinions, the Godzilla brand was soon losing its bite. One online discussion group even included a list of 63 fundamental flaws within the movie (typical example: 'Godzilla can outrun helicopters but he can't keep up with a taxicab').

1998 was the year the movie industry finally realized the influential power of the Internet had over the movie-going public. Not only did it play a fundamental role in making sure Godzilla's excessive marketing budget had been a waste of money, but it was also proving (through the example of the Blair Witch Project and its cult online following) that large marketing budgets weren't always necessary in the first place.

Given the critical mauling Godzilla received, it is interesting to note that three years later Sony was receiving much more positive reviews for its summer blockbusters. Quotes from David Manning, the reviewer from the Ridgefield Press, were included on posters promoting the comedies A Knight's

Tale and *The Animal.* Manning referred to Heath Ledger, star of *A Knight's Tale*, as 'this year's hottest new star', and claimed *The Animal* was 'another winner'.

However, in June 2001 *Newsweek* magazine revealed that David Manning didn't exist, and had been invented by an unidentified Sony marketing executive the summer before to put a bit of positive spin on the hit-starved studio's films. Manning's 'reviews' had also made their way onto posters promoting Sony's *Hollow Man* and *Vertical Limit* movies. 'It was an incredibly foolish decision, and we're horrified,' a Sony spokeswoman said at the time. Sadly, David Manning's opinion of *Godzilla* will remain unknown.

Lessons from *Godzilla*

- *Remember that bigger isn't always better.* Everything about the movie had been big – the star, the special effects, the marketing budget, the brand tie-ins – but it hadn't been enough. Ironically, the slogan for the film was 'Size matters'. In this case, it clearly didn't.
- *Don't over-market your brand.* The excessive amount of hype and brand extensions Sony had created for *Godzilla* ended up working against it. As branding guru Tom Peters has put it, 'leverage is good, too much leverage is bad'. This view is supported and expanded by anti-brand guru Naomi Klein who predicts in *No Logo* that 'the current mania for synergy will collapse under the weight of its unfulfilled promises.'
- *Concentrate on the end product.* It is true that branding is often more about perception than reality, but if your end product is truly awful the brand perception will always be negative.

7 Persil Power

One stubborn stain on Unilever's reputation

In the mid-1990s, the total UK market for soaps and detergents was worth £1.42 billion (US $2.6 billion), and the largest sector was fabric washing, worth £960 million and 67.5 per cent of the total sector. The competition between the two leading companies within the sector, Unilever and Procter & Gamble, was intense and led to a quest for more and more and more innovative brand offerings.

When Unilever's star brand Persil announced the launch of a powerful new formula, aptly called Persil Power, many consumers got excited by the product's apparent ability to fight any stain. However, when the product hit the market place in May 1994, it proved so powerful that under certain conditions it didn't only destroy stains, it destroyed clothes as well.

For the first few weeks though, Persil Power proved successful. Indeed, for a brief period, the product overtook its main rival Ariel. Indeed, Unilever stated that Persil Power represented a 'revolutionary' breakthrough in detergents, and was 'the most significant thing we've ever done.'

The only problem was, the brand's key asset – a patented manganese component called an 'accelerator' which was put in the powder – also proved to be its fatal flaw. As soon as stories of disintegrated clothes started to emerge, Procter & Gamble ploughed their resources into an accusation-laden publicity campaign which not only damaged Persil Power, but also had implications for Unilever itself. Consumers soon understood that the product could damage materials at high temperatures, and that if they bought Persil Power they risked destroying their clothes.

Niall Fitzgerald, who introduced Persil Power (and is now Unilever's chairman) explained the brand damage to the whole Anglo-Dutch company in an interview with *The Sunday Times*. 'Communications had evolved so fast that within seconds this wasn't a brand issue, this was a corporate issue,' he said. 'So even if we had wanted to ring-fence our product, we couldn't have.' Most retailers quickly took the product from their shelves, and Unilever embarked on a massive crisis management programme, together with a complete overhaul of the company procedures that had resulted in the product emerging on the market.

At the start of 1995 Unilever replaced Persil Power with Persil New Generation. The overall cost was estimated at more than £200 million.

Now, however, the whole episode is almost forgotten in the UK customer's mind, and Unilever has bounced back with its launch of detergent tablets. Indeed, the Persil brand has now regained leadership from Procter & Gamble's top brand Ariel.

Ultimately, Unilever has been preserved by its heritage. After all, this is the company which produced the world's first packaged, branded laundry soap, Sunlight, over 100 years ago. Its brands may come and go, but Unilever itself has stayed strong.

Whether this will always be the case is another matter. In 2002, the company announced that it was considering branding some of its products, such as Persil, under its own name. In other words, the product would be branded as 'Persil from Unilever', instead of simply 'Persil'. In an article in the *Guardian* journalist Julia Day explained the logic behind the move:

The idea is to create consumer-friendly brand values – such as a commitment to the environment – for Unilever to use when marketing its products.

Niall Fitzgerald, the chief executive of Unilever, said the company believed the time may be right to develop Unilever as an 'umbrella brand' for its individual products.

The company has avoided taking this route in the past because of the high risk involved. If one product encounters a problem the image of other products could be damaged [. . .]

But the advantages for Unilever are that it could develop Unilever as a brand with 'values' that could be applied to all brands.

One example Niall Fitzgerald gives in the article was establishing Unilever's environmental credentials. 'The cost of doing that for individual brands is immense,' he said.

As the Persil Power episode illustrates, this is a risky move. If, in 1994, the new brand had been branded clearly as 'Persil Power from Unilever', it would have tarnished all Unilever brands, and the damage would have been even greater.

Lessons from Persil Power

- *Don't fuel your competitor's publicity.* Procter & Gamble's negative campaign against Persil Power helped to boost its Ariel brand of detergent.
- *Test products in all conditions.* Products need to be tested in every environment or context they are likely to be used. If Unilever had been able to spot the fundamental flaw with the product it would have prevented what the then Unilever chairman Sir Michael Perry referred to as 'the greatest marketing setback we have seen.'
- *Accept that no brand is an island.* 'Even if we had wanted to ring-fence our product, we couldn't have,' admitted Unilever chief executive Niall Fitzgerald.

8 Pepsi

In pursuit of purity

Coca-Cola may have one of the most famous brand failures of all time, but its long-standing rival has also had its fair share of marketing mishaps.

For instance, in 1992 Pepsi spotted what it considered to be a gap in the market. What the world was waiting for, the company decided, was a clear cola. After all, there had already been a variety of diet colas, cherry colas, sugar-free colas, caffeine-free colas, caffeine-enhanced colas, and all had achieved at least some form of success. So why not a clear cola?

After months of tests and experiments the company arrived at its new, clear formula and decided to call it Crystal Pepsi. They also produced a diet version – Diet Crystal Pepsi. Both products, Pepsi believed, answered the 'new consumer demand for purity.' After all, this was a time when consumers were starting to opt for a bottle of Evian or Perrier just as often as they were picking up a bottle of Coke or Pepsi.

The only problem was that a product with the word 'Pepsi' in its name was expected to taste like, well, Pepsi. But it didn't. In fact, nobody seemed to know *what* it tasted of.

Anyway, after a little more than a year, Pepsi halted the production of Crystal Pepsi and started work on a new clear formula. In 1994, the reworked product appeared on the shelves, branded simply as Crystal, and available only in regular. However, the negative associations persisted and Crystal mark two did even worse than its unpopular predecessor. Pepsi eventually admitted defeat and scrapped the whole concept of clear cola. But never one to give in easily, Pepsi remained aware of the 'new consumer demand for purity.' In 1994, the same year it launched Crystal, Pepsi decided it wanted a piece of the growing bottled water market. It therefore launched its own bottled water product, entitled Aquafina, which had considerably more success than Crystal in the US market.

In addition to Crystal, there have been other, more general marketing problems for Pepsi over the years. In particular, it has had trouble differentiating its brand identity from Coca-Cola. As it wasn't the first to market the cola category, Pepsi was never going to be the generic name. People rarely say, 'I'm going to have a Pepsi'. Even when they have a Pepsi bottle in their fridge they would be more likely to say, 'I'm going to have a Coke.'

However, although this situation couldn't be avoided, Pepsi's branding for many years failed to give the product a stand-alone identity. Crucially, Pepsi breached what Al and Laura Ries refer to as 'The Law of the Color,' one of their 22 Immutable Laws of Branding in the book of the same name. As they state:

> There is a powerful logic for selecting a color that is the opposite of your major competitors [. . .] Cola is a reddish-brown liquid so the logical color for a cola brand is red. Which is one reason why Coca-Cola has been using red for more than a hundred years.

> Pepsi-Cola made a poor choice. It picked red and blue as the brand's colours. Red to symbolise cola and blue to differentiate the brand from Coca-Cola. For years Pepsi has struggled with a less-than-ideal response to Coke's colour strategy.

Recently, though, Pepsi has sacrificed red for mainly blue to create a stronger distinction between the two leading brands. Now Coca-Cola equals red and Pepsi equals blue.

Lessons from Pepsi

- *Don't assume that gaps should always be filled.* If you spot a hole in the market, it doesn't mean that you should fill it. Just because clear cola didn't exist, it didn't mean it had to be invented. However, the previous success the company had with its Diet Pepsi product (the first cola of its kind) had convinced Pepsi that there were more gaps to fill.

- *Don't relaunch a failed product.* Crystal failed once, but Pepsi still believed the world was crying out for a clear cola. The second version fared even worse than the first.
- *Differentiate yourself from your main competitor.* For years Pepsi's visual identity was diluted through its red and blue branding.

9 Earring Magic Ken

When Barbie's boyfriend came out of the closet

Among toys, Mattel's Barbie is something of a legend. Since her arrival on the scene at the annual Toy Fair in New York in 1959, Barbie has appealed to several different generations of girls. One of the keys to her longevity has been her ability to move with the times. In the 1980s, for instance, Barbie wore shoulder pads and became an aerobics instructor. According to the Barbie Web site, she has always set a successful example: 'She has been a role model to women as an astronaut, a college graduate, a surgeon, a business executive, an airline pilot, a presidential candidate and a dentist.'

However, on her road to international superstardom Barbie has experienced a number of setbacks. For instance, when the doll launched in Japan sales were poor owing to the fact that Japanese parents thought her breasts were too large. Mattel addressed the problem and a year later a flatter-chested version emerged.

Then there's Ken, Barbie's perma-tanned boyfriend. Like Barbie herself, Ken has been made over a number of times since his 'birth' in 1961. The most controversial of these incarnations occurred in 1993 with the arrival of 'Earring Magic Ken' or, as he became publicly known, 'New Ken.' This was, to put it mildly, a radical new look for the doll. Gone were the tuxedos of old, and in came a mesh t-shirt, a purple leather vest and a left-side earring. 'It would seem Mattel's crack Ken redesign team spent a weekend in LA or New York, dashing from rave to rave, taking notes and Polaroids,' one journalist wrote at the time of the launch.

Mattel explained that the new look was an effort to bring Ken up to date. 'We did a survey where we asked girls if Barbie should get a new boyfriend or stick with Ken,' explained Lisa McKendall, Mattel's manager of marketing and communications. 'They wanted her to stay with Ken, but wanted him to look. . . cooler.'

However, pretty soon 'New Ken' was being dubbed 'Gay Ken'. The *New York Times*, CNN, *People* magazine and talk-show host Jay Leno saw the doll as a symbol of shifting gender and sexual identities and values. Ken, whose apparent purpose in life was to help define the conventional ideal of masculinity for generations of young girls, had apparently come out of the closet.

This hadn't been Mattel's intention. 'Ken and Barbie both reflect mainstream society,' said Lisa McKendall. 'They reflect what little girls see in their world – what they see their dads, brothers and uncles wearing they want Ken to wear.'

Of course, Mattel was now positioned 'between a rock and a hard place'. A 'gay' doll aimed at children was not going to do them any favours among middle America. However, if they acted too appalled by the associations they risked being accused of homophobia.

Crunch-time came when columnist Dan Savage published an article for gay-oriented newspaper *The Stranger*, which said that 'Earring Magic Ken' included too many signifiers of gay culture for it to be coincidental. 'Remember the sudden appearance of African-American Barbie-style dolls after the full impact of the civil rights movement began to be felt?' Savage asked his readers. 'Queer Ken is the high-water mark of, depending on your point of view, either queer infiltration into popular culture or the thoughtless appropriation of queer culture by heterosexuals.'

Savage went even further, slamming Mattel's statement that Ken was representative of the relatives of the little girls who took part in the research: 'What the little girls were seeing, and telling Mattel was cool, wasn't what their relations were wearing – unless they had hip-queer relatives – but the homoerotic fashions and imagery they were seeing on MTV, what they saw Madonna's dancers wearing in her concerts and films and, as it happens, what gay rights activists were wearing to demos and raves,' he wrote.

Following this article, and the interest it caused, Mattel discontinued the Ken dolls and recalled as many as they could from the shelves. Ken's brush with controversy was now over and Barbie could sleep easier knowing her boyfriend was still interested in her.

Lesson from Earring Magic Ken

- *Research children's markets carefully.* Mattel asked five-years-olds how they wanted Ken to look. And they told them. But that didn't mean parents were going to buy the new-look Ken dolls when they finally emerged.

10 The Hot Wheels computer

Stereotyping the market

A computer aimed specifically at children may seem like a good idea. Patriot Computers certainly thought so, which is why they came up with the Hot Wheels PC in 1999. These computers, which came with Intel chips and Windows 98 software, were targeted primarily at the boys' market and the hardware was decorated with racing car imagery including the Hot Wheels flame logo. In addition, Patriot Computers had made a deal with Mattel to produce a Barbie computer aimed at girls. The boys' computer was blue, the girls' was pink with a flowery pattern.

Both products flopped. One of the reasons, according to analysts, was the crude attempt at gender marketing. Pamela Haag, director of research at the American Association of University Women's Educational Foundation, told the *Wall Street Journal* that this type of marketing was 'very out of step with what adult men and women are doing, and therefore with what children want – it really is anachronistic.'

Justine Cassel, professor at the MIT Media Lab and co-author of *From Barbie to Mortal Kombat*, also thought the computers were crudely conceived. 'Just because you cover a traditionally boy product with girlish clichés doesn't guarantee girls will like it,' she said.

The computers were also criticized as bad cases of surface design trying to save a standard product. 'It was just a desktop computer with some stickers on it,' wrote *Business 2.0*. Shortly afterwards the products flopped. Patriot Computers went bankrupt.

Lessons from the Hot Wheels computer

- *Don't resort to stereotypes*. Dressing up a computer with stereotypical gender specific imagery was not enough to entice children or their parents.
- *Get designers involved at the start*. 'To avoid such costly flameouts, designers should be involved with projects from the outset, giving engineers input on product usability and interface issues,' advised *Business 2.0*.

11 Corfam

The leather substitute

In the mid-1960s, chemical giant DuPont invested millions in the promotion of Corfam, a synthetic substitute for leather. But although Corfam was launched in 1963, it had been conceived many years before. Indeed, in the late 1930s researchers at DuPont had discovered ways to make leather-like materials and had experimented with various possible uses. One of the most obvious uses was for footwear. Demographic trends were starting to indicate that the global population was increasing at such a rate that there would soon be a demand for footwear from non-animal sources.

DuPont therefore believed the world would greet the arrival of their hard-wearing, shine-preserving, water-repelling leather look-a-like. And indeed, when the product made its first public appearance at the Chicago Shoe Show in the autumn of 1963, it was greeted enthusiastically.

All DuPont had to do now was to find out where exactly Corfam's place in the footwear market would be. The company had predicted that by 1984, a quarter of US shoes would be made from Corfam, but to do that it would first need to carve a niche for itself. In the United States of 1963, the footwear market could be divided into the following percentages:

47 per cent	Women's shoes
20 per cent	Children's shoes
18 per cent	Men's shoes
15 per cent	Athletic footwear/Other

Clearly if Corfam was to become as big as it could be, it would need to be used by manufacturers of women's shoes. It soon became clear, however, that the female shoe market was itself divided – between comfy, everyday shoes and 'fashion' shoes made for special occasions.

For all Corfam's strengths, it was not as flexible or 'skin-like' as ordinary leather, and therefore was not suited for those shoes designed for comfort or everyday use. So fashion shoes seemed to be the solution. And yet, even here there was a problem. A synthetic material called polyvinyl chloride (now known to us as PVC) was fast becoming popular owing to its extreme low cost. Vinyl shoes, which could be coloured or embossed very easily, were perfect for women looking for a 'throwaway' pair which may be worn once or twice at special occasions before being discarded.

Furthermore, the leather industry was keen to dampen the appeal of Corfam by lowering its prices and improving quality. This factor, combined with the growing popularity of vinyl shoes, led to DuPont's announcement in March 1971 that they were to withdraw Corfam. On 11 April 1971, the *New York Times* referred to Corfam as 'Du Pont's $100 million Edsel.'

Lessons from Corfam

- *Improve on the original.* For a substitute product to work it needs to be better than the original in the minds of consumers. Although Corfam was long-lasting, it lacked the flexibility and 'breathability' of leather. It also proved too expensive.
- *Remember that there's no such thing as a certain success.* Corfam was, without doubt, one of the most thoroughly researched and developed products of all time. As such, DuPont felt that its prediction that by 1984, 25 per cent of US shoes would be made of Corfam, was a justifiable one. And yet, Corfam wasn't even around to see 1984, having failed after just seven years.
- *Compete on quality or value.* When a product is unable to be the best in terms of either quality or value it faces an uphill struggle to convince consumers of its merits.

12 RJ Reynolds' smokeless cigarettes

The ultimate bad idea

Cigarette manufacturers have often thought that the best way to build market share is to come up with new twists on the standard cigarette formula. For instance, Marlboro has had dozens of different varieties in its history, including Marlboro Menthol, Marlboro Lights and Marlboro Medium.

Normally, cigarettes produce new varieties based on different levels of tar. For instance, in the UK the Silk Cut brand produced various low-tar varieties – Mild, Low and Ultra Low. The popularities of such low-tar brands has caused cigarette companies to think of ever more ways to try and convince consumers that their unhealthy and anti-social products aren't as unhealthy or as anti-social as they might have thought. Similar strategies have been deployed in the beer market, with brands such as Bud Light, Coors Light and Miller Lite.

However, some of these strategies take an extreme form. For instance, in the alcohol market there was the case of the beer brand which tried to sell beer-branded mineral water. The brand was Coors. The water it produced was called Coors Rocky Mountain Spring Water. It was launched in 1990 and survived only two years.

In the cigarette industry, the extreme strategy belonged to RJ Reynolds Tobacco Company known for brands such as Camel, Winston, Salem and Doral. In 1988, when the anti-smoking lobbyists could finally claim the majority of public opinion was behind them, and when passive smoking had been officially recognized as a serious danger to health, the company decided to conduct trials on a smokeless cigarette. In total, RJ Reynolds spent US $325 million on creating a smokeless cigarette which it branded as 'Premier'.

However, problems became apparent straightaway. First, there was the taste issue. One person who 'smoked' Premier complained that it 'tasted like shit'. And he was RJ Reynolds' chief executive.

Then there was the difficulty of using the product in the first place, as *Reporter Magazine* (www.robmagazine.com) explains: 'Inhaling the Premier required vacuum-powered lungs, lighting it virtually required a blowtorch, and, if successfully lit with a match, the sulphur reaction produced a smell and a flavour that left users retching.'

In addition, there was the damaging rumour that the smokeless cigarette could be used as a delivery device for crack cocaine. Hardly the kind of brand association RJ Reynolds had wanted to create.

One of the major forms of controversy was the brand's possible appeal among younger people. Here is an extract from a statement by many leading US health organizations shortly after RJ Reynolds announced the new project:

> The American Cancer Society, American Heart Association, and American Lung Association have filed a petition with the US Food and Drug Administration (FDA), asking that Premier be regulated as a drug. In filing this petition, we are not calling for an outright ban on Premier. We want simply for it to be properly tested before people use it.

> We are especially concerned that Premier's intriguing high-tech design will lure children and teenagers into the web of nicotine addiction. RJR's marketing emphasis on 'clean enjoyment' also may lull people who already smoke into a deceptive sense of safety when they really ought to give up the habit altogether.

> According to the FDA, any product marketed that claims that it is healthier or safer, must be regulated by the FDA. Conventional cigarettes escape FDA scrutiny because they are promoted for the sheer pleasure of smoking and because the FDA does not consider them to be drugs or food.

In introducing Premier, RJR is stepping beyond that loophole. The RJR claim that Premier is 'cleaner' is a poorly disguised way to imply 'safer' to thousands of people concerned about the health risks of smoking. RJR knows that if their ads said 'safer' in place of 'cleaner' the FDA would step in.

In the meantime, RJR promises that Premier is an improvement over conventional cigarettes that burn with foul-smelling smoke. But, we are sceptical. How can we trust the same industry that still refuses to admit that cigarette smoking is harmful?

The real problem though was that smokers didn't enjoy using the smoke-free product, and non-smokers didn't have a reason to. In short, there was no market. After four months of very slow sales, RJ Reynolds cut their losses and Premier was withdrawn.

But the story doesn't end there.

By the mid-1990s, concerns about passive smoking led the company to believe there was still a market for smokeless cigarettes. In 1996 it therefore spent a further US $125 million on developing an updated version, this time called Eclipse.

In a press statement, a company spokesman announced the potential appeal of the brand. 'I think we can all agree that for many non-smokers and for many smokers, second-hand smoke is an annoyance, and to be able to reduce and almost eliminate that annoyance is a very positive step in the right direction.'

The new cigarette made less smoke than standard cigarettes because it didn't burn. Instead charcoal was used to heat the tobacco. The user drew heated air over the tobacco to release a tobacco and nicotine vapour. As a result, the Eclipse cigarette caused only 10 per cent of the normal level of cigarette smoke, and promised lower levels of tar and nicotine.

However, whether the cigarette actually lowered the health risk of smoking – either for deliberate or passive inhalers – remains questionable. Sorrell Schwartz, a pharmacologist from Georgetown University who researched the tobacco industry, believed the cigarettes could be good news. 'If it is as smoke-free as it's claimed to be, then clearly the individual's risk of lung cancer, emphysema, bronchitis would be reduced,' Schwartz told CNN. But Schwartz's Georgetown colleague, Dr Naiyer Rizvi, was more sceptical.

'There are risks that may be related to increasing carbon monoxide in this cigarette and heart disease,' he told the CNN reporters.

An independent study commissioned by the Massachusetts Department of Public Health found that when it was compared to ultra-low tar cigarettes, the Eclipse cigarette had higher levels of several toxins, especially when the charcoal tip burned very hot from heavy smoking.

This information was clearly damaging to the Eclipse brand, because from the start the marketing activity was designed to accentuate the health angle. Indeed, the original campaign was to include this pitch. 'The best choice for smokers who worry about their health is to quit. But Eclipse is the next best choice for those who have decided to continue smoking.'

This marketing message provoked opposition from many leading US health organizations. The American Lung Association issued a statement saying, 'we fear that RJR's health claims that this device is "safe" or "safer than cigarettes" may discourage smokers from quitting.'

The Campaign for Tobacco-Free Kids joined the attack, with the organization's president, Matthew L Myers releasing the following statement: 'RJR's announcement that it plans to market a safer Eclipse cigarette is taking advantage of the regulation gap created by the US Supreme Court's decision to remove FDA authority to regulate tobacco. Without FDA oversight, there is no scientific corroboration of these claims by an independent government agency.'

Particularly controversial was the fact that many of the medical experts who had suggested that these cigarettes were less dangerous than standard brands had been doing research paid for by the tobacco company itself. Furthermore, independent medical analysts soon discovered that Eclipse cigarettes presented one health risk which was actually worse than standard cigarettes – glass fibres. John Pauly, from the Department of Molecular Immunology at the Roswell Park Cancer Institute in Buffalo, New York, discovered that 99 out of every 100 Eclipse cigarettes have glass fibres within their filters. These fibres, he told ABC News, were 'invariably' inhaled or ingested when smokers took a drag from an Eclipse.

However, despite this massive outcry from health authorities, including the US Surgeon General, the real reason Eclipse failed to ignite the market was because consumers still felt absolutely no desire for a smokeless cigarette.

Lessons from smokeless cigarettes

- *Don't baffle consumers with research.* RJ Reynolds spent a great deal of money researching the health aspects of its two brands of smokeless cigarettes. However, this only resulted in mixed messages. Although RJ Reynolds' research concluded that in many ways the brands were safer, they couldn't be considered entirely safe. 'As we all know, no cigarette is safe,' admitted RJ Reynolds' CEO Andrew J Schindler. Furthermore, RJ Reynolds' research prompted opposition from other health authorities who published their own independent findings. Rather than end up looking as if it was acting in the public's health interests, the tobacco firm only ended up looking manipulative.

- *Don't sell ice cubes to cocker spaniels.* Smokeless cigarettes appealed to people who didn't like the smell of smoke. These people are called non-smokers, and generally tend not to buy cigarettes. Robert McMath in *Business 2.0* likened this approach to 'trying to sell ice cubes to cocker spaniels,' and asked the seemingly obvious question: 'Why create a product for a consumer who wants nothing to do with you?'

- *Realize that if it has failed once, it will fail again.* RJ Reynolds should have abandoned the whole idea once the Premier cigarette failed.

13 Oranjolt

The drink that lost its cool

Rasna Limited is one of the leading soft drinks companies in India, and made its name in the concentrate market. However, when it has tried to stray from its specialized niche, it hasn't had much success. When Rasna experimented with a fizzy fruit drink called Oranjolt, the brand bombed even before it could take off. Oranjolt was a fruit drink in which carbonation was used as a preservative. 'It was never meant to be a fizzy drink,' says Rasna's founder Piraz Khambatta. He explained that given the threat of foreign competition it was important to try out new things. 'If you don't try new initiatives, you are stuck,' he says. So why did it fail? Because it was out of sync with retail practices.

To last, Oranjolt needed to be refrigerated. The problem was that Indian retailers tend to switch off their shop refrigerators at night. As a result, Oranjolt faced quality problems. The product has a shelf life of three to four weeks where other soft drinks were assured a shelf life of over five months.

Servicing outlets was also a problem. 'We didn't have a distribution structure that could allow us to replace the product every three to four weeks,' admits Khambatta. Even Coke and Pepsi make replacements only once in three months. Oranjolt was therefore launched in select outlets and could not expand rapidly.

That was the only effort by Rasna Limited to try its hand beyond its bread-and-butter segment where it still enjoys over 80 per cent of the concentrated soft drink market share. 'Now we are trying to reinvent the category and expand it,' says Khambatta. 'And we want to be one up over our competition on all parameters.'

Lesson from Oranjolt

- *Cover all bases*. Rasna failed to anticipate the quality problems it faced as a result of retail practices.

14 La Femme

Where are the pink ladies?

In the 1950s, US car manufacturers discovered a new target customer, the female car buyer. Up until that point, cars had been viewed as a male preserve. However, an increase in prosperity combined with the levelling of the sexes that occurred in the years following World War II managed to change all that.

Women wouldn't want any old car though. Oh no. They'd want a car that appealed to their feminine interests. They'd want flowers. They'd want a girly name. They'd want accessories. But most of all, they'd want pink.

At least, that is what car manufacturers Chrysler believed after researching this apparently strange and exotic creature. The end result was La Femme, part of the Dodge division and the first car designed specifically for women. The car was pink and white, and the seats were decorated with a tapestry style cloth depicting a pattern of pink rosebuds on a pink background. The carpeting was dark burgundy colour. In the publicity material La Femme was said to be 'designed for Her Royal Highness – the American Woman.'

In 1955 Dodge sent the following letter, expressing the company's enthusiasm for La Femme, to all Dodge Dealers across the United States:

TO ALL DODGE DIRECT DEALERS:

The enclosed folder will introduce you to the La Femme, by Dodge, the first car ever exclusively designed for the woman motorist.

At the Chicago Auto Show, the La Femme received exceptionally enthusiastic response and it is enjoying similar response at special shows and exhibits in other parts of the country.

Exterior color scheme of the car is Heather Rose over Sapphire White, and there is a gold La Femme nameplate on each front fender, replacing the Royal Lancer nameplate. The interior consists of specially designed Heather Rose Jacquard Fabrics and Heather Rose Cordagrain bolster and trim. The materials used, of course, possess the usual qualities of durability, beauty, economy, and ease of cleaning.

The crowning touches which personalize the La Femme are its special feminine accessories. Two compartments located on the backs of the front seats are upholstered in Heather Rose Cordagrain. The compartment on the driver's side contains a stylish rain cape, fisherman's style rain hat and umbrella which carry out the Jacquard motif. The other compartment holds a stunning shoulder bag in soft rose leather. It is fitted with compact, lighter, lipstick and cigarette case.

Available only in the Custom Royal Lancer model, the La Femme can now be ordered for March delivery. Naturally, a model of this type will initially be built in limited quantities and will be handled on first come, first served basis. Complete price information can be obtained from a Confidential Price Bulletin, which you will be receiving within the next few days.

I hope you will endeavor to see the La Femme at your earliest opportunity. I believe you will agree that this unusual car has great appeal to women, and that it gives Dodge dealers a 'drawing card' enjoyed by no other dealer group.

Very truly yours,
L F Desmond, General Sales Manager Dodge Division

The experiment was a complete failure. The dealers that decided to order La Femme found that the cars sat unsold in the showroom.

Unperturbed, Dodge tried again the following year. But still it had no takers. Women found the crude attempts to attract their attention rather patronizing. This was, after all, appealing to a classic male ideal of femininity, rather than how the 1950s woman actually saw herself. There simply weren't enough women who wanted a pink and purple car with matching lipstick holders and combs.

Lesson from La Femme

- *Don't patronize your customers.* It didn't work in the 1950s, and it certainly doesn't work now.

15 Radion

Bright orange boxes aren't enough

Many of the brands in this section have failed because they were too far away from what the consumer wanted, but sometimes products fail because they aren't different enough from other popular products. This is certainly the case of Radion washing powder. Along with Pear's Soap, Radion was one of the many Unilever brands for the chop when the Anglo-Dutch conglomerate announced it would be narrowing its scope on 400 'power' brands.

Launched 10 years before the February 2000 announcement, Radion had struggled to capture just over 2 per cent of the UK detergent market. One of the reasons for this, as with most brand failures, is that the public's perception of the brand was far from clear.

Although the product's vibrant design (Radion came in shocking orange packets) meant that the brand was easily identifiable on supermarket shelves, consumers were less than sure why they should buy it. It wasn't the cheapest, it wasn't considered the best quality, it wasn't the oldest or the original. It was simply the brand with the brightest packaging. And that, in the end, is rarely enough.

Unilever's final decision was to amalgamate Radion into its brand, and it continues under the banner Surf Fun Fresh.

Lesson from Radion

- *Be different.* Brands need to have a strong point of difference from their competition. After all, this is the very point of branding in the first place. Garish packaging was not enough to win over consumers.

16 Clairol's 'Touch of Yoghurt' shampoo

Launched in 1979, Clairol's yoghurt-based shampoo failed to attract customers largely because nobody liked the idea of washing their hair with yoghurt. Of those who did buy the product, there were even some cases of people mistakenly eating it, and getting very ill as a result. The 'Touch of Yoghurt' concept is made even more remarkable by the introduction three years earlier by Clairol of a similar shampoo called the 'Look of Buttermilk.' This product had instantly bombed in test markets where consumers were left asking: what exactly is the 'look of buttermilk' and why should I want it?

17 Pepsi AM

In the late 1980s, Pepsi spotted a previously unexploited consumer: the breakfast cola drinker. Although Pepsi hadn't conducted much comprehensive market research into this area, the company realized that many young adults were drinking caffeinated cola rather than coffee for breakfast. They therefore came up with Pepsi AM, a drink 'with all the sugar and twice the caffeine.'

Unfortunately, Pepsi had failed to appreciate that although some people drank Pepsi for breakfast, there was no specific demand for a new sub-brand centred around that usage. 'If a consumer doesn't know he [or she] has a need, it's hard to offer a solution,' says brand expert and marketing author Robert McMath. 'Sometimes a company can manufacture a need – but it's expensive that way.'

Nobody knew they wanted Pepsi AM, so nobody bought it. Furthermore, many marketing experts have successfully argued that because its name dictated when the product should be consumed, the market size was restricted to specific-occasion usage. Another bad idea, another flop.

18 Maxwell House ready-to-drink coffee

General Foods launched cartons of Maxwell House ready-to-drink coffee in 1990. The cartons, which appeared in the refrigerated sections of supermarkets, declared the product represented 'a convenient new way to enjoy the rich taste of Maxwell House Coffee.' The packaging stated that the coffee was brewed with 'crystal clear water,' and promised that the 'fresh brewed flavour and aroma are locked in this exclusive foil-lined fresh-pack.' The cartons also had a convenient screw-on plug to aid ease of use. The only trouble was the product couldn't be microwaved in its original container. Therefore the key incentive to buy ready-to-drink coffee – convenience – was taken away. As no-one fancied drinking cold coffee, the product failed.

19 Campbell's Souper Combo

Another attempt at making life more convenient was soup manufacturer Campbell's 'Souper Combo' idea, consisting of a combination frozen soup and sandwich. Designed for people with microwaves at the office or 'latch-key kids' cooking for themselves on their own at home, the product apparently fared well in tests.

The company spent millions on generating awareness for the 'Souper Combo' sub-brand, and the initial sales results were quite encouraging. However, it soon became clear that these were from people making one-off purchases, trying the product out of sheer curiosity. Consumers realized that despite the claims of increased convenience, it was actually quicker and easier to open a can of soup and make your own sandwich than prepare a Souper Combo. They therefore didn't buy the product again.

20 Thirsty Cat! and Thirsty Dog!

Bottled water for pets

The worst of all bad ideas must surely be the Thirsty Cat! and Thirsty Dog! brands of bottled water designed for pampered pets. Although the water came in such 'thirst-quenching' flavours as Crispy Beef and Tangy Fish, pets and their owners remained unimpressed.

CHAPTER 4

Extension failures

Barron's *Dictionary of Business Terms* defines brand extension as 'the addition of a new product to an already established line of products under the same name.'

Okay, so that's the definition – but what's the incentive? Many companies believe that once they have created a successful brand, they should extend it into other product categories. After all, it is not the product that makes a brand, but rather an association. For instance, IBM doesn't simply make computers, it offers 'solutions'. As such, it has been able to enter related categories such as software and networks.

However, although brand extension may increase sales in the short term, it can devalue the identity of the brand in the long term. And when that happens, every product that falls under the brand name starts to suffer. As marketing experts Jack Trout and Al Ries have argued throughout most of their writing careers, line extensions cost market share. In the United States, 7-Up cut its share of the market in half when it added brand variations such as 7-Up Gold. 'Invariably, the category leader is the brand that is not line extended,' argues Jack Trout. However, if properly executed, extensions can work. For instance, in 1982 Coca-Cola launched Diet Coke. Today, it's the third most popular cola drink and boasts over a billion dollars worth of sales every year. Gillette razors and shaving cream are a further example of a successful extension. But when companies fail to understand the true nature of their brand the results can be disastrous.

Of course, the reasons for brand extension are obvious. When a company has saturated a market with one product, it has two options for growth. Either it can expand into a new market or launch a new product. If it goes for the latter option, there are economic reasons for using the same brand name. After all, the extension results in immediate consumer recognition, less money spent on advertising (required to generate awareness of the name), and increased visibility of the parent brand. Costs are saved further if extension can use the same distribution network as the original product.

Then there are the examples of successful brand extensions that encourage other brands to follow suit. Of these, Virgin is the most obvious. 'Brands are built around reputation, not products,' says Richard Branson. Yet even Virgin has proved considerably more successful in some categories than others. Virgin Cola, for instance, proved a complete flop. Furthermore, Virgin has built its reputation as the consumer's champion, entering significantly different markets (bridal wear and pensions, for example) without diluting its identity. The consumers' perception of Virgin is also unified by the charismatic figure of Richard Branson himself. Think Virgin, and it's not too long before you think of Branson. So while the Virgin product and service offerings broaden year by year, the brand identity remains coherent.

Most other brands, however, do not have such versatility. For instance, Volvo has built up its reputation around the notion of 'safety'. If it was suddenly to launch a car without airbags, it would contradict its established brand identity.

And yet, despite the danger involved, brand extensions are everywhere. Nine out of ten new grocery products are line extensions. Think also of the beer market. US beer drinkers 25 years ago had a choice of three major brands – Miller, Coors and Budweiser. Today there are over 30 varieties of these same brands, yet the number of beer drinkers remains roughly the same.

Having said that, most of the brands which boast successful extensions have moved into related categories. Coca-Cola had a global hit when it launched Diet Coke. It was less successful however when it introduced its own range of clothing. Gillette is often celebrated as a great 'how to' model for brand extension. It moved smoothly from selling razors to selling shaving cream. With such compatible products the success of one product feeds the success of the other, and the brand as a whole feels the benefit.

Often however, extensions have been made by companies with no apparent understanding of what their brand is about. Many believe they can have their cake and eat it, that having built a strong brand perception based around one product category, they can transfer it to unrelated products and increase sales on the back of the same brand name. Other companies that may have a better understanding of their brand identity may still weaken their brand assets by launching products so similar that they cannibalize their original market. As the examples over the next few pages serve to illustrate, both approaches result in failure.

21 Harley Davidson perfume

The sweet smell of failure

In various magazines, at various conferences, and in his online newsletter, Saatchi and Saatchi's worldwide chief executive officer, Kevin Roberts, has talked of the 'mythology of the brand'. The most powerful brands, according to Roberts, are those that have built their own mythology, or rather, that have helped their loyal customers to build this mythology. The one brand with perhaps more mythology attached to it than any other is, without doubt, Harley Davidson.

Harley Davidson owners aren't just loyal. They *love* the brand. They do not care that the motorcycles they ride are not the best in terms of technology or that they may be prone to the occasional oil leakage. What matters is the biker myth – the freedom of the open road, and all its macho connotations.

This myth is vividly conjured up in the book *Hell's Angel: The Life and Times of Sonny Barger and The Hell's Angels Motorcycle Club* by Sonny Barger (the original Hell's Angel). In a chapter entitled, 'Harleys, Choppers, Full Dressers and Stolen Wheels,' Barger writes:

> What it's really about with a Harley Davidson is the sound. . . everybody loves that rumble. Another thing Harley owners really crave about their bikes is the low-end torque, the raw power coming out of the gate. It runs out pretty quick once you get up past ninety miles an hour. Most

Harley riders don't care about high speed, they'd rather have that low-end torque, the one that gurgles down in your groin and gives you the feeling of power. The Japanese bikes, while they *have* the power, they don't quite have the *feeling* of power.

The appeal of the Harley Davidson is essentially masculine and its customers take brand loyalty to extreme levels. Indeed, many testosterone-charged Harley owners even tattoo the Harley Davidson name and imagery onto their bodies.

The company has attempted to capitalize on this unique strength of feeling towards the brand, by pushing the Harley Davidson chain of shops selling a wide variety of branded merchandise – Harley Davidson T-shirts, socks, cigarette lighters and ornaments. While Harley Davidson's core fans may have accused the company of 'Disneyfying' the brand, the real problem occurred when Harley Davidson attached its name to a range of aftershave and perfume. For lovers of the motorcycle, this was an extension too far. Harley Davidson had fallen into the trap of thinking that more products equals more sales. And it usually does, at least in the short term. But as Al and Laura Ries write in *The 22 Immutable Laws of Branding*, this type of strategy can have negative consequences in the long term:

Do you build the brand today in order to move merchandise tomorrow? Or do you expand the brand today in order to move the goods today and see it decline tomorrow? [. . .]

Line extension, megabranding, variable pricing and a host of other sophisticated marketing techniques are being used to milk brands rather than build them. While milking may bring in easy money in the short term, in the long term it wears down the brand until it no longer stands for anything.

Ironically, though, this quest for more products and to broaden the Harley Davidson line went against the way the company had built the brand in the first place. In *Hell's Angel*, Barger writes:

Harley has enjoyed a huge share of the large bike market for decades. They control about fifty percent of cruiser sales, with Japanese bikes making up the other half. As a result, they often act a little high and mighty toward their customers.

An official at Harley Davidson was once quoted as saying, 'Enough bikes is too many, and if we make enough, we lose mystique.' While they keep saying they're building more and more each year, up until a couple of years ago I believe Harley Davidson intentionally held back production to stir up demand.

The implication is that Harley Davidson originally understood that its customers could have too much of a good thing. Not only had it stayed focused on motorbikes, but the company may have also limited their availability in order to generate the Harley Davidson 'mystique'.

By the 1990s, however, the brand was clearly heading in the other direction. Alongside aftershave and perfume, the company also launched Harley Davidson wine coolers. As you would expect, the bikers were not impressed.

On her Internet homepage, one biker girl, who calls herself 'Tinker', recounted her experience of seeing all these inappropriate items on sale in a Harley Davidson chain store:

Drifting closer, I found myself dazzled by the seemingly infinite variety of stuff. Man, they had everything under the sun! There were H-D socks, perfumes, infant clothes, an entire line of kids wear, tons of ornaments and collectables, even ties, all stamped with the official H-D license logo. Everything, from the truly nice to the frankly ugly, was on display. Everything that is except an actual Harley Davidson motorcycle. No parts, even. There was a Buell [a Harley Davidson model] in the window, with a 'Do Not Touch' sign on it.

A salesperson wandered over. 'Can I help you find something?' she asked brightly.

'Sure,' I said. 'Have you got the official licensed Harley Davidson shampoo?'

'Shampoo?' she asked, a little uncertain.

'Oh absolutely,' I said. 'It looks and smells just like motor oil, but it makes my hair so manageable!' I smiled as I made my escape, but I know it's just a matter of time.

Tinker was not alone in her criticism. And pretty soon, it became clear that the motorcycle giant was alienating its core customers.

'Harley Davidson values are strong, masculine, very rugged values,' says Charles E Brymer, chief executive officer of the Interbrand Group, a branding consultancy based in New York. 'For Harley Davidson to go into a sector that doesn't live up to what those values are would be disastrous.'

However, the disaster was a relatively limited one. The company has now admitted its mistake, and stopped producing perfumes and other inappropriate products.

In an interview for *The Business Knowledge Network*, Joe Nice, the director of corporate communications for Harley Davidson, spoke candidly of the company's branding failures. 'Over the years,' he said, 'we're tried a number of different approaches to merchandising and put the Harley Davidson brand on some things that, in retrospect, we may not have been well-advised to do. The company is much more selective today about who we work with and how we go about extending the brand.'

Lessons from Harley Davidson

- *Focus on your brand values.* If your values are 'strong, masculine and very rugged,' you shouldn't be selling perfume or wine coolers. A range of baby clothes may also be a bad idea.
- *Don't alienate your core customers.* For brands that inspire strong loyalty, the temptation is to test that loyalty to its limits by stretching the brand into other product categories. However, this is a dangerous strategy and can lead to what marketing experts refer to as 'brand dilution' – in other words, a watered-down brand.
- *Remember that more is less.* 'When you study categories over a long period, you can see that adding more can weaken growth, not help it,' writes Jack Trout in his book, *Big Brands, Big Trouble: Lessons Learned the Hard Way*. 'The more you add, the more you risk undermining your basic differentiating idea, which is the essence of your brand.'

- *Keep it tight.* Harley Davidson built its brands by staying true to what it does best, namely making big, classic, US motorbikes. The further it moved away from this original focus, the further it got into trouble. Any brand which attempts to be a 'Jack of all trades' will ultimately fail to carve a strong identity in any category.
- *Handle 'lovemarks' with care.* According to advertising guru Kevin Roberts, truly successful brands don't have 'trademarks'. They have 'lovemarks'. In a now famous article for *Fast Company* magazine's September 2000 issue, Roberts cited Harley Davidson as a supreme example of a lovemark and commended the company for not following the marketing rulebook. Although Roberts says that the motorbikes themselves are 'actually pretty average', the nature of the brand has meant that the motorbikes don't have to be compared to others in terms of performance. Roberts says:

> As a lovemark, Harley Davidson has two things. One is its signature rumbling sound. The other is that you can't go very fast on a Harley, so you have to ride in a pack [. . .] The mystery of the Harley isn't in its performance, and it isn't in any of the words that end in 'er'. Most brands are built on 'er' words – faster, bigger, better, cleaner. Mystery doesn't need those words. Mystery also doesn't need hundreds of themed stores to push its brand extensions. In fact, such an approach tends to erode the mystery altogether.

22 Gerber Singles

When branding goes ga ga

Baby-food manufacturer Gerber is responsible for one of the most frequently referenced brand failures of all time. Alongside Coca-Cola's New Coke and Harley Davidson's perfume, Gerber's attempt to crack the adult food market is certainly one of the main entrants in the branding Hall of Shame.

The idea was to produce small servings of food for single adults – such as fruits, vegetables, starters and desserts – in the same jars used for baby food. However, when Gerber's adult range was launched in 1974, the company soon discovered that the idea of eating products such as 'Creamed Beef' out of a small jar was not most people's idea of a good night in.

Furthermore, the product was called Gerber Singles. According to Susan Casey in the October 2000 issue of *Business 2.0*, 'they might as well have called it I Live Alone and Eat My Meals From a Jar.'

Whether the product had been market researched is anybody's guess – and it is certainly hard to get a comment from Gerber itself. One thing is certain, however. Baby food for grown-up loners failed spectacularly.

Lesson from Gerber Singles

- *Think from the consumer's perspective.* Although Gerber Singles made sense from Gerber's perspective (after all, the company could save manufacturing costs by using the same jars as for its baby food), no consumer was interested in buying a product which not only told the world that he or she couldn't find a partner, but also gave the reason why (because the person was a big baby).

23 Crest

Stretching a brand to its limit

Born in 1955, Crest was the first fluoride toothpaste brand. Up until that point, the Colgate brand had a stranglehold on the market.

However, Crest's parent company Procter & Gamble realized that Colgate had a weakness. No fluoride. This meant more cavities and more tooth decay. Furthermore, Crest could back up miraculous cavity-reducing claims with extensive research, which had been conducted by Procter & Gamble scientists at Indiana University. Endorsements by the American Dental Association, which commended Crest's 'effective decay-preventing qualities,' helped the brand gain ground on its rival, Colgate, and eventually saw it slide ahead.

However, the 1980s witnessed the fragmentation of the toothpaste market. All of a sudden, consumers were presented with an array of choice as new brands emerged. There were brands for smokers, tooth-whitening brands, mint-gel brands, baking-soda brands, natural brands, children's brands, flavoured brands, brands for the elderly. Furthermore, fluoride was no longer such a big selling point. After all, in many parts of Europe and the United States it was now included in tap water. Cavities weren't the issue they were in the 1950s.

Gradually, Crest launched more and more varieties. Most significantly, it released a tartar control toothpaste in 1985. Although this was the first toothpaste of its kind on the market it didn't have the same impact as the introduction of fluoride had 30 years previously. One of the reasons for this was that Crest now had so many different toothpastes. The anti-tartar variety was just one Crest among many. Also, Colgate was quick off the mark. Not only did it launch its own tartar-control toothpaste, but it also started work on a toothpaste which would cover all of the perceived tooth care needs.

Whereas Crest kept on offering new variations on the same theme, thereby confusing the toothpaste-buying public, Colgate launched Colgate Total. This came with fluoride, tartar control and gum protection. In other words it provided everything within one product. Soon after its triumphant launch, Colgate was back on top of the market and eating into Crest's sales.

So what happened? Why wasn't Crest able to offer a Crest Total or Crest Complete before its rival's product?

There are a number of possible reasons, and one relates to Procter & Gamble's method of branding. Procter & Gamble's brand strategy in the 1980s seemed to be: why launch one product, when 50 will do? Indeed, at one point there were 52 versions of Crest on the market. The belief was: the higher number of sub-brands the higher number of sales. So why risk threatening this scenario by telling consumers there is now one Crest toothpaste which caters for all their dental requirements?

However, increased choice equalled increased confusion. As a result, Crest lost market share. Indeed, true to the law of diminishing returns the more products Crest had on offer, the lower its overall share of the market. When Crest had one product, its share soared above 50 per cent. By the time Crest had 38 products it was down to 36 per cent of the market. As soon as there were 50 Crest toothpastes, its market share dipped to 25 per cent and fell behind Colgate.

These problems were not unique to the Crest brand. For instance, Procter & Gamble had seen the same thing happen with its Head & Shoulders brand. Did consumers really need 31 varieties of anti-dandruff shampoo?

When the marketing strategy firm Ries & Ries went to work for Crest, they identified this problem. In *The 22 Immutable Laws of Branding* Al and Laura Ries recount the experience:

When we worked for Crest, the marketing manager asked us, 'Crest has thirty-eight stock-keeping units. Do you think that's too many or too few?'

'How many teeth do you have in your mouth?' we asked.

'Thirty-two.'

'No toothpaste should have more stock-keeping units than teeth in one's mouth,' we responded.

Although for some time Procter & Gamble kept on repeating the misguided Crest strategy – launch more brands, lose more market share – the company eventually decided to tackle the problem it had created.

An article entitled, 'Make it Simple', *Business Week* magazine (9 September 1996) summed up the decisive shift within Procter & Gamble: 'After decades of spinning out new-and-improved this, lemon-freshened that, and extra-jumbo-size the other thing, Procter & Gamble has decided that it sells too many different kinds of stuff. Now it has started to do the unthinkable: it's cutting back. Procter's product roster is a third shorter today than it was at the start of the decade.'

Before it cut the number of Crest products, Procter & Gamble trimmed back on hair care. Having slashed the number of its hair care items in half it saw an increase in sales. However, according to Procter & Gamble's chief executive of hair care Robert S Matteucci, the strategy was unpopular at first: 'The moves met some resistance from Procter & Gamble's brand honchos who thought, "Oh my God, we're going to lose sales because we're going to have fewer items,"' he said at the time the decision to trim back was made. 'There's a huge scepticism that this is the right thing to do, and that it's doable.'

As well as reducing the number of Crest toothpaste varieties, Procter & Gamble also altered the Crest package design to make it simpler to find your favourite version of the product. The move was considered an intelligent one among marketing experts. In a 1998 Ithaca *American Demographics* survey, Marcia Mogelonsky applauded the new strategy: 'This reduces the number of extraneous sizes, flavours, and other variants, making it easier for consumers to find what they want. At the same time, the manufacturer can have more of its allotted space in the store filled with its best-selling products. Shoppers have less choice, but they are less confused, and the manufacturer makes more money.'

However, competition remains tough. Not only from Colgate, but also Aquafresh, Mentadent, Arm and Hammer, Sensodyne and own-brand ranges such as those produced by the UK chemist Boots.

Although Procter & Gamble has simplified the Crest range to some degree, and although sales have improved, some believe it isn't enough to usurp Colgate. Furthermore, although Procter & Gamble has honed its range, some critics claim that Crest's brand identity is still not sharp enough and that it has neglected its scientific origins. For instance, in his book *Big Brands, Big Trouble*, Jack Trout makes the following observation:

> First and foremost, Crest should always be on the serious, therapeutic side of the toothpaste market. That's where they are in the minds of their prospects. No mouthwash, no whitening, only serious tooth care technology. The natural evolution of Crest would be to move from 'cavity prevention' to becoming the 'pioneer in tooth care'. Unfortunately, they never quite saw this as a way to go. They continued to tinker with different forms of Crest.

The fact that Procter & Gamble hasn't always been focusing on tooth decay has meant that it has inevitably suffered from something even worse: brand decay. Unless the company can once again take control of the scientific high ground and provide consumers with a single, consistent message (assisted with a tightly-focused range), Colgate will have won the battle by more than the skin of its teeth.

Lessons from Crest

- *Don't confuse the customer.* Procter & Gamble now realize that simplicity is the key to reassuring shoppers. 'It's mind-boggling how difficult we've made it for them over the years,' admitted Procter & Gamble's president Durk I Jager to *Business Week* magazine.
- *Don't offer too many products.* Just 7.6 per cent of all personal care and household products account for 84.5 per cent of sales, according to research by the consulting firm Kurt Salmon Associates. The same research discovered that almost a quarter of the products in a typical supermarket sell fewer than one unit a month.
- *Remove product duplicates.* Another study, published by William Bishop Consulting, found that when duplicative items were removed, 80 per cent of consumers saw no difference.
- *Be transparent.* Brands should aim for 'transparency'. In other words, they should make the choice on offer completely clear.
- *Remember your heritage.* 'Never lose your corporate memory,' advises Jack Trout in *Big Brands, Big Trouble*. Crest suffered from brand amnesia by failing to replicate the success of its 'Triumph Over Tartar' campaign of the 1950s.

24 Heinz All Natural Cleaning Vinegar

Confusing the customer

Heinz's All Natural Cleaning Vinegar was the food-maker's first non-food item. The company, which had been founded by Henry Heinz in 1869, had made its name selling its '57 Varieties' – good value, pre-packaged food such as baked beans, soup and ketchup – and decided in the 1980s to extend its brand into other household goods.

First off the mark was the All Natural Cleaning Vinegar, an eco-friendly, all-purpose vinegar carrying a red symbol with the words 'Heloise's Most Helpful Hint'. Heloise is the US newspaper columnist responsible for the 'Hints from Heloise' column, which is syndicated across the globe. It was a logical endorsement as Heloise had long been an advocate of the various and miraculous uses of vinegar – as a rust remover, deodorizer, window cleaner, ant detergent, weed killer and defroster. In addition to this support, the product also received a substantial amount of positive PR from the press, which had picked up on the green angle of the product.

None of this mattered though. The product was a complete flop and never appeared beyond the United States.

When marketing commentators attempted to explain why the vinegar had failed to take off, they blamed the 'alternative' perception of the new product. In her 1998 book, *Green Marketing: Opportunity for Innovation* Jacquelyn Ottman uses the case of the Heinz All Natural Cleaning Vinegar to illustrate the changing market attitudes towards environmentally-friendly products:

'With green a moving target, planning gets tricky; industry can only respond as quickly as the market demands. This poses the risk of rushing greener products to market to serve the demands of influential customers while mass consumers may be unaware of the need for change. The green marketplace is rife with examples of less than perfect timing.'

Ottman then goes on in depth to explain why she believes the Heinz product failed:

> Introduced in response to the newly discovered need of chemophobics, Heinz's Cleaning Vinegar, a double-strength version of the normal product, flopped when introduced into supermarkets as an alternative cleaning aid. The mass consumer didn't know what to make of it. While greater consumer marketing and educational efforts no doubt would have helped enhance its chance of success, the product opportunity may have been better served by a niche strategy, distributing the product in health-food stores and green-product catalogs until enough of the mass market was prepared to switch to the ecologically-conscious offering.

However, there is another reason why consumers may have been wary. Heinz was a food brand. If the company produced a vinegar, consumers would expect to be able to pour it over their meals. They didn't expect to find it sitting alongside the bottles of bleach and household detergents.

Of course, for Heinz, the decision to launch the product was a thoroughly logical one. After all, the company already produced vinegar, so why not intensify the strength of that product to create a new one? As Ottman explains in her book, 'many green products on the market today represent small enhancements or tweaks to existing ones.'

But the 'tweaks' to Heinz's original product had moved the brand away from its core identity – namely, that of a food manufacturer. The fact that both vinegar and Heinz are normally associated with things you can eat only made the product more confusing for the customer. In other words, as All Natural Cleaning Vinegar was based on an existing, *edible* Heinz vinegar, the product only served to reaffirm the perception of Heinz as a producer of food.

The only trouble was, the cleaning vinegar *wasn't* food. As a result, it failed.

Lessons from Heinz

- *Stick to what you know.* But more importantly, stick to what your customers know. If you're a food brand that means one thing. If you can't eat it, you can't sell it.
- *Expand within the limits of your brand perception.* Heinz may be most associated with ketchup but it has numerous other brand successes, and frequently launches new products. Heinz shows that you can extend your line as far as you want, providing you remain true to your core identity or brand perception.
- *Adopt a niche strategy for a niche product.* Heinz All Natural Cleaning Vinegar was distributed and marketed as a mainstream product, although it only appealed to a niche market.

25 Miller

The ever-expanding brand

In the 1970s Miller Brewing Company faced something of an image problem. For years it had been positioning its core brand, Miller High Life, as 'the champagne of beers'. Jazz musicians had been used in advertising campaigns to endorse the beer and to consolidate its sophisticated image, but the results were increasingly disappointing.

When *Business Week* profiled the company in November 1976, it explained the problem with Miller's marketing strategy. 'Sold for years as the champagne of beers, High Life was attracting a disproportionate share of women and upper-income consumers who were not big beer drinkers [. . .] A lot of people drank the beer, but none drank it in quantity.'

In order to differentiate itself from its macho rivals, Budweiser and Coors, Miller had feminized its core brand in a bid for wider share of the market. However, the company was starting to learn what Marlboro had realized the decade before when it replaced images of female smokers with the iconic Marlboro Man. The lesson was this: in reaching out to new customers, a brand risks alienating its core market. But help was at hand. Philip Morris, the owners of the Marlboro brand, had purchased Miller at the start of the decade. The company now realized what it had to do.

Just as the Marlboro Man had been an exaggerated image of masculinity, so the new advertising for Miller High Life was designed to out-macho its rivals. Out went the sophisticated jazz musicians, and in came testosterone-fuelled oil workers glugging back the beer like there was no tomorrow above the no-nonsense slogan, 'Now Comes Miller Time.' As the testosterone levels rose, so too did sales, with High Life becoming the second most popular beer by 1977. However, by that time, Miller had another success story on its hands in the form of Miller Lite.

Miraculously, Miller managed to introduce this low-calorie beer without tarnishing its macho image. The ads, featuring leading sports figures and the strap-line 'everything you always wanted in a beer – and less', were very success-ful, and by 1983 Miller Lite was second only to Budweiser in the beer rankings.

Less miraculously, it soon became apparent that the rising popularity of Miller Lite was offset by the declining popularity of High Life. While the introduction of the light beer in 1974 had led to increased overall sales in the short term, in the long term it was costing the company its original brand. Having peaked in 1979 with sales of over 20 million barrels, High Life was now in terminal decline.

What Miller should have learnt from this experience was that the success of one Miller brand was at the cost of another. As marketing expert Jack Trout famously put it, 'in the mind, it's one idea to a brand.' But Miller continued to extend its brand in further directions, and with similar results. In 1986, the company launched a cold-filtered beer called Miller Genuine Draft. Again, the beer was a success. Again, the other Miller brands suffered. By 1991, sales of Miller Lite were starting to decline.

The incentive to launch new brands was still strong, though. After all, every new Miller beer which had emerged on the market increased sales for the company in the short term. And short-term trends were always going to be easier to spot than those which happen slowly, over years and decades.

Rather than create completely new brands, the company kept on launching sub-brands under the Miller name. So whereas their 1970s counterparts were only offered Miller High Life, Miller drinkers in the 1990s had considerably more choice. Walking into a bar or supermarket, they not only had to choose between Miller, Coors and Budweiser, but between various brands within the Miller range itself.

There was still Miller High Life (hanging on by a thread) and Miller Lite, but also Miller Lite Ice, Miller High Life Lite, Miller Genuine Draft, Miller Genuine Draft Lite, Miller Reserve, Miller Reserve Lite, Miller Reserve Amber Ale and the very short-lived Miller Clear. The trouble was not so much that there were too many Miller brands (although that was indeed a problem) but that they were variations of each other, rather than a variation of one core brand. (Incidentally, this theory explains why Diet Coke succeeded where New Coke failed. Whereas the former had supplemented the original brand, the latter had eradicated it completely.)

In 1996 Miller decided to address this situation, adding yet another brand to the mix, Miller Regular. The company had looked at the success of its rivals' regular beers and wanted a piece of the action. In other words, they wanted a beer which would come to represent everything Miller stood for, which by that point was rather a lot.

The only problem was that with so many Miller brands already out there, launching another one (even with a US $50 million marketing budget) was always going to be a challenge, especially when it had such an unassuming name. With an apparently limitless array of Millers to choose from, most people assumed that Miller Regular had always been there. As a result, the brand failed to make an impact and Miller eventually decided to withdraw it altogether.

The problem of identity, however, still remained. Whereas drinkers could go into a bar and say to the bartender, 'I'll have a Budweiser,' causing little confusion, if they said, 'I'll have a Miller,' the bartender would inevitably ask, 'Which Miller?'

As Jack Trout wrote in his excellent and influential book, *The New Positioning*, 'the more variations you attach to the brand, the more the mind loses focus.' Miller hadn't just alienated its core customers, it had completely baffled them. Whereas in the 1970s Miller had achieved its success by tightening its focus, by the time the company had reached the new millennium it had broadened itself beyond recognition.

While Miller's long-standing rival, Budweiser, has now taken its regular brand identity to new levels of simplicity (reflected in the one-word strap line, 'True'), Miller still suffers from a lack of coherence. So, although the beer itself may taste great, the brand has definitely become watered down.

Lessons from Miller

- *Don't extend your brand too far.* 'Leverage is good, too much leverage is bad,' says brand guru Tom Peters. He is joined in this opinion by Al Ries and Jack Trout, for whom 'The Law of Line Extension' is one of 'The 22 Immutable Laws of Marketing.' This law states, 'if you want to be successful today, you have to narrow the focus in order to build a position in the prospect's mind.'

- *Have a core brand.* While Ries and Trout are right to highlight the potential problems of line extension, it is important to differentiate between those companies that can get away with it, and those that can't. Brand extensions aren't bad in themselves. For instance, nobody in his or her right mind would call *Diet Coke* a bad branding decision. Even Miller's chief competitors have played the extension game. In some respects, Budweiser is as guilty as Miller at broadening its line (consider Bud Light, Bud Dry and Bud Ice, for example), but unlike Miller, it has a core brand, Budweiser itself. Miller, on the other hand, has merely become the sum of its many parts. By the time the company tried to rectify the situation, with the launch of Miller Regular in 1996, it had left it too late.
- *Learn from your mistakes.* Miller was clearly too focused on the success of each new brand it created to understand the negative impact these new brands were having on its existing beers.
- *Change your brand name.* Although Miller was launching new brands, it kept hold of the 'Miller' name. If the company had created completely new names for each range, there would have been less consumer confusion.

26 Virgin Cola

A brand too far

Many brands fail when they move into inappropriate categories. For instance, Harley Davidson perfume proved to be an extension too far.

Virgin, however, is one company that seems to be able to apply its brand name to anything. Although Richard Branson's empire began as a record label, signing groundbreaking acts such as the Sex Pistols, it now encompasses virtually everything – from airlines to financial services.

An article which appeared on 27 August 2000 in the UK newspaper *The Observer* explained the way in which members of the public can 'live a Virgin life':

> Every morning you can wake up to Virgin Radio, put on Virgin clothes and make-up, drive to work in a car bought through Virgin using money from your Virgin bank account. On your way home you can pop into a Virgin Active gym. At weekends you can use a Virgin mobile phone or Virgin's Internet service to find out what is on at the local Virgin cinema. As you head off on holiday on a Virgin train or plane, you can play Virgin video games stopping only to buy your Virgin vodka in duty free. If you meet someone on the beach and one thing leads to another, the Virgin condoms are in the Virgin hotel minibar. When love blossoms, you get married with Virgin Brides and buy your first house with a Virgin mortgage and get a joint Virgin pension.

In most cases, these brand extensions are successful. However, sometimes even Branson, dubbed 'the people's capitalist', can stretch himself too far.

In the mid-1990s, the scale of his ambitions for the Virgin brand became clear. 'I want Virgin to be as well-known around the world as Coca-Cola,' he was quoted as saying. So what better way to achieve this goal than to enter the cola market itself. He therefore decided to join forces with Cott Corporation, a Canadian private-label soda maker, to produce cola under the Virgin name. In doing this, he was placing his brand with what he referred to as the 'cola duopolists'. Namely, Coca-Cola and Pepsi.

Immediately, the move raised eyebrows among those who knew the market well. 'It would be easier to make a snowman in July in Florida than to take on Coke and Pepsi,' observed John Sicher, publisher of the US trade publication, *Beverage Digest*. But Branson seemed to relish the challenge, launching the drink to the US market in spectacular style. He rode a vintage Sherman tank through New York's Times Square, aiming fire at a huge Coca-Cola billboard. He also placed his own 40-foot Virgin Cola billboard right above the Times Square Virgin Megastore. 'The signage alone was worth the rent of the entire building,' he joked at the time. 'The store is a bonus.'

However, the new cola brand struggled on both sides of the Atlantic. Although it was priced 15–20 per cent lower than the two leading brands, not enough consumers were being won over. Part of the problem was distribution. Coca Cola and Pepsi managed to block Virgin from getting crucial shelf space in half the UK's supermarkets. Meanwhile, Coke doubled its advertising and promotion budget. As Rob Baskin, Coca-Cola USA's spokesman said: 'We take all competition seriously.'

Ultimately, Coca Cola and Pepsi's hold on the market has proven too strong and Virgin Cola failed to make a serious dent in their worldwide sales. Even on Virgin's home turf, the UK, the brand struggled to gain 3 per cent of the market and it has never made a profit.

Lessons from Virgin Cola

- *Strong brands depend on exploiting competitors' weaknesses.* 'We often move into areas where the customer has traditionally received a poor deal, and where the competition is complacent,' Branson once said, explaining Virgin's brand strategy. However, Pepsi and Coca Cola are anything but complacent.
- *Distribution is everything.* If you can't get the product on the shelves, it will never outsell its competitors.

27 Bic underwear

Strange but true

Harley Davidson perfume. Coors spring water. Both of these were doomed to failure because of the brand name's attachment to an unrelated product. However, the prize for the most bizarre brand extension must go to Bic.

The company, best known for producing disposable pens, thought its brand name was strong enough to be applied to other categories. Indeed, it had already achieved success with disposable cigarette lighters and safety razors. The unifying factor here was 'disposability'. Bic pens, lighters and razors were all throw-away goods. Furthermore, Bic could exploit its well established distribution network and sell the lighters and razors in the same outlets as its pens.

However, when the Bic brand applied its name to women's underwear, consisting of a line of 'disposable pantyhose' they were unable to attract customers. Okay, so the disposability element was still there. But that was about it. Consumers were unable to see any link between Bic's other products and underwear, because of course there was no link.

The main problem was that the company insisted on using the Bic name. As marketing writer Al Ries has observed, using the same name in unrelated categories can create difficulties. 'If you have a powerful perception for one class of product, it becomes almost impossible to extend that perception to a different class,' he argues. 'Names have power, but only in the camp in which they have credentials and when they get out of their camp, when they lose focus, they also lose their power.' Although this doesn't hold true for every brand – Virgin is an obvious exception (and one Ries rarely discusses) – it certainly holds true in this instance.

Furthermore, Bic underwear required a completely new distribution channel and required different production technology. The lighters, razors and pens were all made from injection-moulded plastic, and could therefore share resources. Production and distribution problems, combined with the fact that the product's function was totally unlike that of the previous products, meant that Bic underwear met an early, and not much-mourned death.

Lessons from Bic underwear

- *Exploit existing resources.* The other Bic brand extensions made sense because the company could exploit its existing sales force, distribution channels and production technology. None of which came in handy for the range of underwear.
- *Be flexible.* The brand association for Bic in the mind of the consumer simply wasn't flexible enough for a move into an unrelated product category.

28 Xerox Data Systems

More than copiers?

Xerox is one of the branding success stories of the 20th century. As with many other similar successes, the company didn't just create a product, it invented a whole new category. Indeed, such is Xerox's achievement that its brand name has become a part of everyday speech. In the United States, xerox is a verb, used when people are copying paper.

Chester Carlson was the man who started it all. In 1928, he invented plain-paper copying, a process he referred to as 'xerography' (a term based on the Greek words for 'dry' and 'writing'). But it wasn't until 1947 that 'xerography' became a business, as well as a technological, venture. That was when the New York-based Haloid Company met with Carlson and acquired the licence to develop a xerographic machine. One year later the words 'Xerox' and 'xerography' had been patented.

1949 saw the launch of the first ever Xerox machine, called simply Model A. A few years later the Haloid company had changed its name to Haloid Xerox and in 1959 it introduced the product which was to put Xerox on the map. The Xerox 914 was the first automatic plain-paper copier and, as such, attracted considerable media attention. Indeed, within months of its launch *Fortune* magazine was writing enthusiastically about this machine, which could make over seven copies a minute, and referred to it as 'the most successful product ever marketed in America.'

Word spread about this amazing product, and very soon it was becoming an office essential. The company, rechristened the Xerox Corporation in 1961, was now listed on the New York Stock Exchange. By 1968, company sales rose to the US $1 billion mark. In 1969, Xerox became a majority shareholder of the European operation, Rank Xerox, and so the Xerox name was now a truly global brand.

The following year, the company strengthened its reputation as a technological innovator by setting up the Xerox Palo Alto Research Center, abbreviated as Xerox PARC. However, the research centre was also a testimony to Xerox's broader ambitions. From 1970, the company expressed its desire to stretch beyond copying into the field of computer technology and data processing. In 1975 this desire became a reality with the launch of a computer product, Xerox Data Systems, which had been researched at Xerox PARC. It failed disastrously and Xerox lost US $85 million. Four years later though, the company was still determined to extend its brand beyond the copier market, this time with an early version of a fax machine called a Telecopier. Another disastrous failure.

The problem wasn't that Xerox's brand name was too weak. On the contrary, the problem was that Xerox was a very strong brand name, but one associated almost exclusively with copier machines. Xerox wasn't just a company that made photocopiers – it *was* photocopiers. It didn't matter if the machine was made by Canon or Kodak, people still referred to it as a Xerox machine. Indeed, this was an impression enforced through Xerox's own marketing efforts. Through much of the 1970s and 1980s Xerox ads used to pose the question: 'How to tell the real Xerox from a Xerox copy?' The implication was that if it wasn't Xerox, it wasn't the real thing. While this strategy helped to sell copiers, it meant that it was tied to that product category. After all, no one brand can claim to be the only genuine article in more than one category.

For years, Xerox had competed on the superior quality of its copier products. Then, when the company's rivals had caught up, it competed on the superior quality of its brand. And as soon as a company makes the transition from a simple product manufacturer, to a global brand, it has to live with the consequences. It can't just create a strong perception and then undermine that perception by embarking on other categories. As Al Ries memorably put it, 'the difference between brands is not in the products, but in the product names. Or rather the perception of the names.'

However, Xerox didn't give up. Instead, it tried to tackle the problem head on. For instance, in a magazine ad for Xerox Computer Services, the strap line read: 'This is not about copiers.' But of course, this only confirmed the impression that Xerox *was* about copiers.

During the 1980s, Xerox tried to reposition itself as a provider of all technology-based office products. At the start of the decade, the company launched a personal computer, or (as Xerox preferred to term it) an 'information processor'. Again, there was nothing fundamentally wrong with the product, at least for the time. But again, the product failed. Similar failures occurred when Xerox tried to launch office networks such as the XTEN network and the Ethernet office network, which were designed to compete with IBM's Satellite Business network. Both the Xerox networks failed to make an impression.

Despite its best efforts to be associated with office technology, the public remained stubbornly unwilling to think of Xerox in any terms other than office *copier* technology. Although the company had invested fortunes in creating office information systems, this was an area steadfastly linked to another technology brand – IBM.

So why, then, did Xerox persist in trying to reposition its brand during the 1980s? Part of the answer may lie in the company's admiration for Japanese models of business. It had close links with Fuji, and had a unique insight into the Japanese management style. In Japan, brand extension was, and indeed remains, the norm, especially for technology companies. For instance, there are few areas of home entertainment where the Sony brand doesn't dominate. Yamaha is another example of successful brand extension. Although the company started producing pianos in the 19th century, it has not been tied down to musical instruments. After 60 years of piano-making, the Japanese company moved into various other product categories with very little difficulty. Think Yamaha and what do you think? Pianos? Organs? Motorbikes? It is most likely that you think of all three.

Other Western companies have also been influenced by the Japanese approach to branding. Take Virgin, for example. Richard Branson has been famous for criticizing brands such as Mars, which refuse to attach the name to other types of products.

What I call 'Mars Syndrome' infects every marketing department and advertising agency in the country. They think that brands only relate to products and that there is a limited amount of stretch that is possible. They seem to have forgotten that no-one has a problem playing a Yamaha piano, having ridden a Yamaha motorbike that day, or listening to a Mitsubishi stereo in a Mitsubishi car, driving past a Mitsubishi bank.

However, among Western companies Xerox remains more typical than Virgin. Unlike Xerox, Virgin doesn't risk brand dilution. As John Murphy, chairman of the international branding consultancy Interbrand once observed: 'Unless they poison someone or start applying the brand to inappropriate products such as pension funds or photocopiers, I doubt whether the Virgin brand will ever be diluted.'

In 1996 Murphy had to eat his words when Virgin did start to move into pension funds. However, there is little sign that Virgin is about to compete with Xerox in the photocopier market. Even Richard Branson might have a problem reversing the intrinsic association the Xerox name has with the product it invented.

The simple fact is that most large brands are associated with one product or service offering. With Coca-Cola, it's cola. With Levi's, it's blue jeans. With McDonald's, it's fast food. And with Xerox, it's copiers.

Xerox was never going to be a Virgin or a Yamaha, but it still kept trying. Recognizing this fact, brand expert Jack Trout, president of Trout and Partners, advised Xerox to concentrate on what it did best. Trout realized that Xerox could remain within the copier market and still be at the forefront of technology. The solution? Laser technology. As Trout has since written about the experience:

> There I was, facing a room full of technical and marketing people who were dutifully executing the office automation strategy that had been in force for years. I was the designated outside messenger bringing the bad news that all their past efforts were in vain and they should focus on the lowly laser printer instead of their glorious office machines. This was not a popular message.

Indeed, Trout soon realized that Xerox believed the future lay in another direction:

> To this day, 15 years later, I have a vivid memory of an interchange that ended this meeting. After listening to my impassioned plea about laser printing, an engineer in the back of the room stood up and said that laser printing was 'old hat'. Xerox had seen the future and it was about to be 'ion deposition'. I asked what that was. The reply was that it was a little hard to explain to a layperson, but it was going to be fast and cheap. My response went something like this, 'When that happens, we

can move to ionography, but for now let's jump on the laser and lasography.'

So what happened? According to Trout, 'the room went icy cold, the sale was lost, and another prediction was pursued that never happened.'

Indeed, the strategy which followed that disastrous meeting cost Xerox billions. Although the company now seems to accept its fate as a 'copier brand', it spent years exploring other, profitless avenues. As a result, competitors such as Canon and IBM have made serious inroads into the copier market, with their high-speed machines. However, providing Xerox can keep its focus on copiers and direct its technological ambitions towards this narrow, but still lucrative market, it could still dominate in the future.

Lessons from Xerox

- *It's vital to know who you are.* Xerox's major mistake lay in trying to transform itself into an IBM-style 'information business'. The rest of the world kept on viewing Xerox as a company which made photocopying machines.
- *Nobody knows the future.* George Orwell's novel *1984* tells us more about the period it was written in than the year 1984. Likewise, future business and technological predictions rarely come true. For instance, no-one predicted the rise of SMS text messaging on mobile phones. Xerox spent too much time and energy looking into a future which didn't exist.
- *Brands are bigger than products.* 'The most valuable asset of the US $19.5 billion Xerox Corporation is the Xerox name itself,' says Al Ries. That name, however, is exclusively and historically associated with copier machines. It doesn't matter that Xerox PARC has come up with some of the most significant technological developments in computing, such as the invention of the mouse. All that matters is the association of the brand name in the consumer's mind.

29 Chiquita

Is there life beyond bananas?

Chiquita has been associated with bananas since 1944, the year the fruit supplier was founded. Indeed, this was the brand's original intention. Not only to get the public to eat more bananas, but to get them to want to buy only those with the Chiquita sticker on them.

However, in recent times the banana association has been something of a mixed blessing, to say the least. After all, bananas represent only a tiny fraction of the entire fresh produce market (less than one per cent). Furthermore, Chiquita has witnessed rival brands successfully make the transition from one type of fruit into other areas. For instance, after years of careful marketing the Dole brand has managed to shift its core identity away from the product category 'pineapple' towards the more general attribute 'delicious and healthy'. This has meant Dole has achieved equal success with other categories of fruit and vegetables.

In recent years, Chiquita has also tried to move away from its core association, by moving into related categories. For instance, in 1987 the company launched Chiquita frozen juice bars. The experiment was a complete disaster, and according to *Business Week* magazine cost the company over US $30 million.

However, Chiquita hasn't stopped trying. A decade later it launched a range of 'exotic juices' which fared only marginally better. The company has also invested heavily in TV ad campaigns across the United States to inform people that it sells more than just bananas. Indeed, the Chiquita range of fresh produce includes pears, peaches, plums, grapefruits, green vegetables, grapes and cantaloupe. But even after the campaign most consumers and retailers still firmly associated the brand with bananas.

This wouldn't be so bad, if the company's banana sales were booming. But Chiquita was badly hurt towards the end of the 1990s with a number of banana-related problems. Quite simply, there were too many of the damn things. Banana production in Ecuador, the world's leading banana producing nation, more than doubled from 1990 to 1999. This increased supply forced Chiquita to charge lower prices. As a result, the margin of profit diminished and debts mounted.

There were also other problems over which Chiquita had no control. For instance, Hurricane Mitch devastated Chiquita's banana plantations in Honduras and Guatemala in 1998, forcing the company to spend more than US $75 million rebuilding them.

Chiquita has also accused the European Union of favouritism towards Caribbean bananas grown in former European colonies. The long-running dispute hit Chiquita hard and according to Stephen G Warshaw, president and chief operating officer of Chiquita, the company had about a 40 per cent share of the European market before 1993, but that dwindled to 20 per cent. Although the EU banana trade policies were changed in 2001, Warshaw is sceptical that the company will be able to regain the dominant market position it once held.

The problems affecting the banana industry, combined with unpaid debts resulting from expansion and its many attempts to broaden its product offering, means the Chiquita brand is now in deep trouble. Whether the brand's fortunes will be able to curve back up, banana-style, remains to be seen.

Lessons from Chiquita

- *'Catch-22' situations should be avoided.* Chiquita tried to stretch its brand when banana sales were slipping. This led the company into debt, because it wasn't selling enough bananas to cover costs. It needed to move beyond bananas to bring in more money, but more money was needed to move beyond bananas. A classic 'catch-22'.
- *Historical identities are hard to shake off.* The company has been linked with bananas since the 1940s and that association has been difficult to undo.

- *A brand is never under total control.* The development of a brand is only ever predictable to a certain extent. Some factors will always be beyond control. Chiquita's expensive attempts at diversification left the brand ill-prepared to cope with unavoidable situations such as Hurricane Mitch, the excessive production of bananas from Ecuador and the Euro's weakness against the dollar.

To understand the risks of brand extensions it is worth taking a brief look at 10 more extension failures.

30 Country Time Cider

Country Time Lemonade Drink was launched in 1976 by Kraft foods as a powder mix, and soon became the top-selling lemonade product sold through US grocery and convenience stores. It successfully extended its line with Country Time Pink Lemonade, which was introduced in 1977. However, when the decision was made to extend the well-known Country Time brand to apple cider, the brand experienced its first failure. Although the brand managers may have thought the brand was chiefly associated with 'good old-fashioned taste' (a Country Time slogan) – an attribute which could be applied equally well to cider – the reality was that the brand simply meant 'lemonade' to most customers.

31 Ben-Gay Aspirin

Ben-Gay is another well-known US brand. It is an analgesic cream used for
the relief of minor arthritic pain, muscle aches and back pain. Again, its first
brand extension – Ultra Strength Ben-Gay – was a success, as it was essentially
the same product, only intensified. When trying to think of another logical
extension, the company came up with Ben-Gay Aspirin. After all, Ben-Gay
could use its existing distribution network and the brand could still be
associated with pain relief. Well, that is what the company thought. The only
trouble was Ben-Gay was so strongly associated with the burning cream that
it was unable to make the transition. Nobody liked the idea of swallowing a
Ben-Gay product. As a result, the Ben-Gay Aspirin failed.

32 Capital Radio restaurants

In November 1996, London station Capital Radio acquired the My Kinda Town themed restaurant company. Rather than keep the My Kinda Town name, the company decided to set up a Capital Radio themed restaurant. As with Planet Hollywood and the Fashion Café, these restaurants were never able to generate enough return custom. Although Capital Radio could boast millions of listeners, very few could see a logical connection between the station and food – because, of course, there wasn't one.

33 Smith and Wesson mountain bikes

In the United States, gun manufacturer Smith and Wesson is a well-known brand. When it decided to capitalize on this wide recognition by launching a range of Smith and Wesson mountain bikes, the company clearly failed to grasp the golden rule of brand extensions. Namely, that the extension must link with the core brand. There needs to be some kind of correlation between the original product (in this case guns) and the extension. Guns and bikes may both be made out of metal, but other than that it is hard to perceive a connection.

34 Cosmopolitan yoghurt

Yes, that's right. *Cosmopolitan* – the world's biggest selling women's magazine – launched its own brand of yoghurt. However, although this extension failed (the yoghurts were off the shelves within 18 months), Cosmopolitan has had success with other crossovers. For instance, Cosmopolitan is now the UK's second-biggest bed linen brand. The connection in this instance is obvious. Namely, sex. There are also plans for Cosmopolitan cafés, which may also fit within Cosmopolitan's 'sex and the city' identity.

'I'm not surprised Cosmo yoghurts failed,' says Jane Wentworth, a senior consultant with the brand consultancy Wolff Olins. 'Any brand extension has to be credible for the mother brand. Companies use brand extensions to reach new audiences and to make the most of their promotional spend – but the important thing is not to tarnish the original brand.'

35 Lynx barbershop

Lever Fabergé, the Unilever division that owns the Lynx brand of male deodorant, opened its first Lynx hairdressing salon in 2000. 'Time and time again, when you ask young chaps in research about Lynx it is the personality of the brand rather than the fact that it is a deodorant that comes out,' said Lynx barbershop project leader, justifying the extension. Promoted as 'bloke heaven' the salons were a post-modern cross between an old-fashioned barber shop and a video games arcade (arcade games and MTV screens were installed to prevent boredom setting in while customers had their hair cut). The salons also carried a full range of Lynx products and branded merchandise. After 14 months, the salons were closed.

'Brand extensions are not simply a sideline for us – we set aggressive targets for all our initiatives,' a Unilever spokesman told the *Guardian* newspaper. 'The barbershops generated a lot of publicity, but failed to meet the targets.'

36 Colgate Kitchen Entrees

In what must be one of the most bizarre brand extensions ever Colgate decided to use its name on a range of food products called Colgate's Kitchen Entrees. Needless to say, the range did not take off and never left US soil. The idea must have been that consumers would eat their Colgate meal, then brush their teeth with Colgate toothpaste. The trouble was that for most people the name Colgate does not exactly get their taste buds tingling. Colgate also made a rather less-than-successful move into bath soaps. This not only failed to draw customer attention, but also reduced its sales of toothpaste.

37 LifeSavers Soda

Invented in 1912, LifeSavers are one of the favourite brands of sweet in the United States. Concentrating on different flavours of 'hard roll candies', the firm produces nearly 3 million rolls every day. Their popularity is also evidenced by the fact that more than 88 million miniature rolls of LifeSavers are given out each year to trick-or-treaters on Halloween. However, when the company produced a fizzy drink called LifeSavers Soda, the product failed even though it had fared well in taste tests. According to one brand critic 'the Lifesavers name gave consumers the impression they would be drinking liquid candy.'

38 Pond's toothpaste

Pond's, the popular brand of face cream, didn't prove to be quite so popular when it applied its name to toothpaste. In a blind test environment, people were not able to differentiate Pond's toothpaste from that of Colgate. However, when the Pond's name and imagery were attached to the toothpaste, no-one was interested. Although Pond's had successfully extended its brand before (into soap products, for instance), these extensions had all been linked by a similar fragrance. 'The main attribute of a toothpaste is taste, this mismatch between taste and fragrance created a dissonance in the minds of consumers,' says Dr M J Xavier, professor of marketing at the Indian Institute of Marketing. 'To most people Ponds was something to do with fragrance and freshness and used for external application only.'

39 Frito-Lay Lemonade

Frito-Lay is the leading brand of salty snacks in the United States. And what do people want to accompany a salty snack? A soft, thirst-quenching drink. So what could be a better idea than Frito-Lay Lemonade? Although it may have been seen like a logical brand extension Frito-Lay Lemonade bombed. After all, Frito-Lay was a brand which made people thirsty, and therefore is the exact opposite of lemonade. From the consumer's perspective the fruity, sweet drink had little connection to other Frito-lay products.

In the old days, brands knew their place. Harley Davidson stuck to motorcycles, Coca-Cola stuck to soft drinks, and Colgate stuck to cleaning our teeth. Now, of course, everything is all mixed up. If modern life wasn't already confusing enough, brands are trying to complicate matters further by creating multiple identities. Sometimes this works. For instance, the Caterpillar clothing range has proved a phenomenal success. Usually, however, brands struggle when they move into unrelated categories. Brand schizophrenia not only aggregates and bewilders consumers, it also devalues the core brand.

CHAPTER 5

PR failures

It can be expected that brands will have at least one crisis in their lifespan. If a brand is well known its crisis can also be expected to make the headlines.

In most cases though, the crisis does not kill the brand. If the company behind the brand acts responsibly and sensitively, the crisis situation can normally be defused. However, if the company fails to do this, the public will be unlikely to forgive. According to one US survey 95 per cent of respondents were more offended by a company lying about a crisis than about the crisis itself. If the company presents the right information, the consumer will respect it for its honesty.

Pepsi-Cola, faced with a syringe discovered in a bottle, ensured that its entire sales force had accurate information to communicate to customers. The press team also relayed this information to the media. As a result, they prevented a bad situation becoming even worse.

Other companies, however, are not so good at handling trouble. They believe the best way to deal with a crisis is to deny its existence. 'Crisis, what crisis?' is their general response. And indeed, this position of denial is exactly what the public have come to expect. Therefore, those companies that are willing to provide the whole truth and nothing but, score points for their open approach.

After all, the key to successful brand management is being able to provide consumers with what they want. Normally, this means providing a good service or product. At a time of crisis however, it means providing the truth.

Although no company should welcome a crisis, the situation presents an opportunity as well as a threat. This is the time to either establish or destroy trust. If a company tells the truth about a negative incident, it is more likely to be believed later on down the line when it is trying to tell consumers about how fantastic its brand is. Public relations is about exactly that; relating with the public, not ignoring them.

In 1999, Dunkin Donuts' parent company, Allied Domecq, started to grow concerned about a consumer opinion Web site when the company realized that it came above the official dot com site on most of the major search engines. Rather than ignore the site in the vain hope it would eventually disappear, Allied Domecq and Dunkin Donuts monitored the 'anti-site' and frequently responded directly to complaints by private e-mail. Unhappy customers were offered vouchers and discounts and even one-to-one meetings with local store managers.

The site that was originally set up by disgruntled customer, David Felton, to vent anger at Dunkin Donuts' poor customer service, soon became a valuable resource for the company. Allied Domecq eventually managed to buy the site from Felton to turn it into an official customer feedback service. Felton later claimed the reason he was willing to sell the site was Dunkin Donuts' positive response to customer complaints and comments. Today, the site is still up and running and providing both company and consumer with a valuable and informative resource.

Dunkin Donuts therefore not only prevented a crisis situation, but also gained a new way to listen to the customer. The examples given throughout the rest of this chapter are of companies who didn't handle their PR so effectively, and as a consequence fanned the flames rather than extinguishing them.

40 Exxon

Don't say a word

Many companies and organizations have had to deal with a crisis during their history. Only a very few, however, come to represent corporate incompetence and irresponsibility through one critical event. Oil company Exxon is among them.

In 1989, the Exxon Valdez oil tanker ran aground and began spilling oil off the coast of Alaska. Within a very short period of time, significant quantities of the tanker's 1,260,000 barrels had entered the water, making it the largest tanker oil spill in US history.

At the moment of impact the ship's third mate, Gregory Cousins, who was not certified to pilot the tanker into those waters, was at the helm. The whereabouts of the captain, Joseph Hazelwood, at the time of the accident was not immediately explained. A Coast Guard investigator had the blood of the captain and the third mate tested for alcohol. The results were that the captain had unacceptably high levels of alcohol in his blood even nine hours after the accident. The captain was later fined and sentenced to 90 days in prison, a sentence many considered 'too light'.

Efforts to contain the oil spill lagged from the start. 'The initial response was inadequate and didn't match the planned, outlined response measures to be taken in a spill,' said Dennis Kelso, commissioner of the Alaska Department of Environmental Conservation. 'As of 24 hours into the spill, we still haven't seen adequate containment.' According to most observers, the company did too little and too late. Not only was the action to contain the spill slow to get going but the company refused to communicate openly with the press. The Exxon Chairman, Lawrence Rawl, was immensely suspicious of the media, and reacted accordingly.

Within hours an army of journalists had arrived to begin extensive coverage. A company spokesman pointed to the existence of procedures to cover the eventuality – procedures which the TV shots belied. When asked if he would be interviewed on TV, Rawl's response was that he didn't have time for 'that kind of thing'.

While the company was getting off to a bad start with the media, the operation on the ground was failing to control the spill. Around 240,000 barrels had been spilled, with another million still on the ship. During the first two days, when calm weather would have allowed it, little was done to contain the spillage. This spillage spread out into a 12 square mile slick.

Then the rain and wind started to make things worse, meaning further containment was near impossible.

A week later the company was still tight-lipped. Following President Bush's declaration that the spill represented a 'major tragedy', Frank Iarossi, the Director of Exxon Shipping, flew to Valdez to hold a press conference. It went badly. Small pieces of good news claimed by the company were immediately contradicted by the eyewitness accounts of the present journalists and fishermen.

John Devens, the Mayor of the Alaskan town Valdez, commented that the community felt betrayed by Exxon's inadequate response to the crisis. 'Over the years, they have promised they would do everything to clean up a spill and to maintain our quality of life. I think it's quite clear right now that our area is faced with destruction of our entire way of life.' Alaskan Lieutenant Governor Stephen McAlpine also said that he was 'severely disappointed' in the company's response. 'Despite all statements to the contrary, I don't think they ever had a handle on it.'

Eventually, the Exxon boss deigned to go onto television. In a live interview he was asked about the latest plans for the clean-up. Rawl started to look nervous. It turned out he had neglected to read these, and cited the fact that it was not the job of the chairman to read such reports. He placed the blame for the crisis at the feet of the world's media. Exxon's catastrophe was complete.

The consequences for Exxon of both the disaster, and the poor way in which it was handled, were catastrophic. The spill cost around US $7 billion, including the clean-up costs. Most of this was made up of the largest punitive fines ever handed out to a company for corporate irresponsibility.

The damage to the company's reputation was even more important, although more difficult to quantify. However, Exxon fell from being the largest oil company in the world to the third largest. The 'Exxon Valdez' became synonymous with corporate arrogance, and the story remained prominent in the media for over a year. According to a 1990 US news poll, 65 per cent of respondents said that 'the Valdez oil spill was the key element in raising public consciousness about environmental issues.'

Lessons from Exxon

- *Live up to your promises.* The company failed to show that it had effective systems in place to deal with the crisis – and in particular its stated ability to move quickly once the problem had occurred was not in evidence.
- *Act like a good corporate citizen.* Exxon acted indifferently to the environmental destruction, and therefore did little to help the company's case.

41 McDonald's – the McLibel trial

As brands go, McDonald's is a biggie. Along with Coca-Cola and Marlboro, it is one of the few brands which is recognized in almost every country. As McDonald's itself proclaims, its chain of fast food restaurants represents the 'most successful food service organization in the world.' There are now approximately 25,000 McDonald's restaurants across the globe, catering for around 40 million people every single day.

The brand reached this position of dominance by arriving at a simple formula, and pushing it hard. As Des Dearlove and Stuart Crainer explain in *The Ultimate Book of Business Brands*, simplicity is the secret behind the brand's success:

> Henry Ford mastered mass product production; McDonald's has mastered mass service production. It has done so through strict adherence to simple beliefs. Quality, cleanliness and uniformity are the basis of the McDonald's brand. [. . .] A McDonald's restaurant in Nairobi, Kenya looks much the same as one in Warsaw, Poland or Battle Creek, Michigan. [. . .] In effect, the very uniformity of the brand is the crucial differentiating factor.

However, by the 1990s McDonald's smooth ride became rather more turbulent. Although it still held onto the crown as king of fast food, the company experienced a number of setbacks. There were new product failures, such as the Arch Deluxe (discussed in Chapter 2), and various run-ins with environmentalists, anti-capitalists and other activists. One of the most notorious, and certainly one of the most protracted of these confrontations was the libel case involving Helen Steel and Dave Morris.

Although the trial didn't reach court until 1994, the case revolved around a pamphlet first published in 1986 by London Greenpeace, a splinter group of Greenpeace International. The pamphlet focused on a variety of social and environmental issues such as animal cruelty, exploitative marketing (in McDonald's advertising campaigns aimed at children), rain forest depletion and the perceived negative health value of McDonald's products.

However, very few people would now know about the contents of that pamphlet if McDonald's hadn't taken the matter to court. Even Naomi Klein, the anti-branding commentator and author of *No Logo,* claims that the pamphlet distributed by Helen Steel and Dave Morris lacked 'hard evidence' and was 'dated' in its concerns:

> London Greenpeace's campaign against the company clearly came from the standpoint of meat-is-murder vegetarianism: a valid perspective, but one for which there is a limited political constituency. What made McLibel take off as a campaign on a par with the ones targeting Nike and Shell was not what the fast-food chain did to cows, forests or even its own workers. The McLibel movement took off because of what McDonald's did to Helen Steel and David Morris.

McDonald's first sought action against 'the McLibel two' over the leaflet in 1990. In fact, the company initially issued libel writs against five activists but three backed down and apologized. For Steel and Morris, however, the threat of legal action also represented an opportunity. The trial could, and indeed did, provide a much larger platform for their views than they would ever have been given standing outside McDonald's restaurants distributing pamphlets.

As it turned out, the trial became the longest in English history, with a staggering total of 313 days in court. And as the trial developed, so too did the media interest. Pretty soon, millions of people knew exactly what was being discussed in that courtroom. Every single statement made in the original pamphlet was discussed and dissected not only in court, but in news studios around the world. In *No Logo,* Naomi Klein highlights the protracted nature of the case:

With 180 witnesses called to the stand, the company endured humiliation after humiliation as the court heard stories of food poisoning,
failure to pay legal overtime, bogus recycling claims and corporate spies
sent to infiltrate the ranks of London Greenpeace. In one particularly
telling incident, McDonald's executives were challenged on the company's claim that it serves 'nutritious food': David Green, senior vice
president of marketing, expressed his opinion that Coca-Cola is
nutritious because it is 'providing water, and I think that is part of a
balanced diet.'

Whichever side of the fence they sat, most commentators agreed on one
thing: the longer the trial went on, the more damaging it was for McDonald's
public image. In any case, the actual facts of the case were too complicated
for most observers to be able to understand clearly – the judge's verdict
document was over 1,000 pages long.

When the verdict was finally announced on 19 June 1997, McDonald's
were able to claim victory as Steel and Morris were ordered to pay damages.
The allegations in the pamphlet linking McDonald's to food poisoning,
cancer and third-world poverty were deemed by the judge as unsupportable.

However, McDonald's was not able to undo the damage caused by the
lengthy trial. On 20 June 1997, the *Guardian* newspaper observed that: 'Not
since Pyrrhus has a victor emerged so bedraggled.' Indeed, although Morris
and Steel were ordered to pay £60,000, this was a low price compared to that
which McDonald's were paying in terms of negative PR (not to mention legal
fees).

For one thing, the original pamphlet – *What's wrong with McDonald's* – had
now become a cult collector's item, with 3 million copies in circulation across
the UK. Then there was the McSpotlight Web site which published all
20,000 pages of the court transcript. The damage was further prolonged
through the publication of John Vidal's widely acclaimed book, *McLibel:
Burger Culture on Trial*. There were numerous TV programmes focusing on
the trial, such as Channel 4's three-hour dramatization, *McLibel*.

So while McDonald's won in court, they lost the media battle. As Naomi
Klein points out:

For Helen Steel, Dave Morris and their supporters, McLibel was never
solely about winning in court – it was about using the courts to win over

the public. [. . .] Standing outside their neighbourhood McDonald's in North London on a Saturday afternoon, Steel and Morris could barely keep up with the demand for 'What's wrong with McDonald's?' the leaflet that started it all.

In the *Guardian*, the UK newspaper that covered the trial from day one, the consequences were also seen to stretch beyond the four walls of the courtroom:

> Consider the cost of this pyrrhic victory. Firstly, the judge upheld several important charges made by the campaigners against the company [. . .] But much more serious was the wide support which the McLibel Two received from the World's media in this epic battle between 'the small fries and the burger giant.' [. . .] Publicly, McDonald's has remained tight-lipped over its pursuit of two unemployed green campaigners with no assets, but somewhere in its empire must be asking some awkward questions. As PR fiascos go, this action takes the prize for ill-judged and disproportionate response to public criticism.

Ultimately, the McLibel trial serves as a reminder to other companies of the importance of 'brand perception'. In the final analysis, the facts didn't matter. What mattered was the way the media's perception of McDonald's influenced a considerable strand of public opinion, and to this day the McLibel trial has left a stain on the company's international reputation.

Lessons from McLibel

- *Don't underestimate the power of the Internet.* Supporters of the McLibel campaign were able to organize themselves online. Brands need to monitor and respond to online criticism in a positive way. 'Things are two-way now,' explains Internet guru Esther Dyson. 'Customers are talking back to companies, employers are talking back to their bosses and vendors are talking back to suppliers.' The Internet manages to bring aggrieved consumers and activists together, in a way that simply wasn't possible in the age of one-way media. In the words of Doc Searles, who co-founded one of Silicon Valley's leading advertising agencies and is a co-author of *The Cluetrain Manifesto*, 'What these little voices used to say to a single friend is now accessible to the world. The speed of word of mouth is now limited only by how fast people can type.' In other words, if people want to get their point across there is little companies can do to stop them.

- *Understand that financial muscle isn't as strong as it used to be.* Following on from the previous point, the power of the Internet means that financial resources are no longer enough to suppress criticism. 'One of the major strengths of pressure groups,' says Peter Verhille, of the PR firm Entente International, 'is their ability to exploit the instruments of the telecommunication revolution. The agile use of global tools such as the Internet reduces the advantage that corporate budgets once provided.'

- *Concentrate on public perception.* In trying to set an example against the Greenpeace activists, McDonald's helped to highlight the activists' cause.

42 Perrier's benzene contamination

No matter how careful a company is, bad things can happen to its brands. The part that is within the company's control is how it decides to handle crises when they occur.

The company most respected for its crisis management capabilities is Johnson & Johnson. When a problem emerges with a Johnson & Johnson brand, the company addresses it immediately, and never tries to cover it up. For instance, when the company learned that its Tylenol brand of painkillers had been tampered with in a US supermarket, the company acted straight-away. It ordered that the Tylenol product be taken off the shelves of every outlet in which it was sold, rather than just the specific supermarket where it had been tampered with.

Once the recall was in effect, Johnson & Johnson announced that it would not put Tylenol painkillers back on the market until the product was more securely protected. This meant making sure Tylenol had tamper-proof packaging, and so the company designed individually packaged pills in foil bubbles. Of course, both the recall and the repackaging cost Johnson & Johnson a lot of money, but this short-term loss was more than compensated by the fact that Tylenol's brand was preserved in the long term. Some experts have argued that the Tylenol brand eventually benefited from the crisis, because consumers were so satisfied and reassured by the company's response.

Not all brand crises are handled so effectively. In 1990 high levels of the toxic substance benzene were discovered in bottles of Perrier. The company had little choice but to recall the product. Within a week the company withdrew 160 million bottles worldwide.

However, when the media first found out about the problem Perrier did not know what to do. For a brand whose whole identity was based around the idea of 'natural purity', the benzene incident was clearly a disaster. Although the recall had been announced straightaway, Perrier's information vacuum started to provoke even more consumer anxiety than there would have been otherwise.

Furthermore, although the company set up a 24-hour hotline in the UK, Perrier refused to see it as a global issue. This was a mistake. As Alex Brummer commentated in the *Guardian* newspaper: 'all politics may be local, but brands are global.' There was a lack of a coherent and consistent response from Perrier subsidiaries, and no lead or co-ordination from the French parent company Source Perrier. Mixed messages were being given, with contradictory and conflicting statements emerging from different divisions of the company. In some cases, the media was even given incorrect information. Perrier therefore made a bad situation worse and failed to tackle the global implications of the crisis.

Of course, the Perrier brand is still fizzing away. Indeed, when Perrier returned to the shelves it was accompanied by the successful 'Eau! Perrier' advertising campaign. However, Groupe Perrier was taken over by Nestlé in 1992, and the brand has still not been able to regain its pre-1990 volume share.

Lessons from Perrier

- *Don't hide the truth.* 'Managing news in crisis, not just wars, is not about trying to suppress bad news – that will lose your credibility,' says Martin Langford, managing director of Burson-Marsteller's corporate and public affairs practice. 'Consumers and journalists are far too smart. You've got to be dead straight with the media because your employees will be if you're not.'
- *Don't breach the consumer's trust.* A brand has been defined as the capitalized value of the trust between a consumer and a company. Breach that trust, and the brand is in trouble.
- *Accept that global brands need coherent communications policies.* A global brand such as Perrier cannot ignore the fact that problems in the United States will be able to impact on sales in Europe. Such a brand needs a

common purpose throughout the organization, so the response to a crisis can be co-ordinated.

- *Recognize that some brands' crises are worse than others.* The benzene contamination was the worst possible crisis to afflict a brand associated with natural purity.

43 Pan Am

Ending in tragedy

In the 1980s, Pan American World Airways, or Pan Am, was one of the most famous brands of airline on the planet. For more than 60 years it had pioneered transocean and intercontinental flying. Having begun life in 1927 with a few aircraft and a single route from Key West to Havana, Pan Am came to represent US commercial aviation policy overseas. However, in the late 1980s the company started to struggle to achieve goals and performance began to slip.

Then, in 1988, disaster struck. A Pan Am plane on route from London to New York disappeared from radar somewhere above Scotland. Later it emerged that a bomb had gone off in the cargo area, causing the aircraft to break in two. The main body of the plain carried on for 13 miles before coming to ground in the small Scottish village of Lockerbie. The total search area spanned 845 square miles and debris turned up as far as 80 miles from Lockerbie. In total, 270 people were killed, including 11 on the ground. One witness told television interviewers 'the sky was actually raining fire.'

The horrific nature of the tragedy, the fact that everybody knew that the airline involved was Pan Am, and also the international nature of the story, meant that the Pan Am name was tarnished and could never recover. Despite the company's constant promises of commitment to increasing its airline's security, the public was simply not willing to fly with Pan Am anymore. After three years of flying with empty seats, in 1991 the company went bankrupt and shut down.

Lesson from Pan Am

- *Some crises are too big to recover from.* Pan Am handled the Lockerbie disaster as best as it could, but the decline in public confidence proved too much.

44 Snow Brand milk products

Poisoning a brand

Among the most dreaded situation for any food brand, an outbreak of food poisoning ranks pretty high. For Snow Brand, Japan's premier dairy foods company, 2000 was the year when that nightmare came true, in the most disastrous way.

After consuming milk or related products made by Snow Brand, 14,800 people, mostly in western Japan, suddenly came down with food poisoning. The problem was traced to bacteria on the production line of Snow Brand's Osaka factory that processed low-fat milk. As soon as the news hit, the brand was in crisis. To make matters worse, the company broke every PR rule in the book and initially sought to downplay the incident. The overall impression Snow Brand gave was of being more concerned for the brand's tarnished image than for the victims of the outbreak.

Perhaps the worst mistake the company made was the effort to limit the extent of the product recall it would have to make. The Osaka city public health centre had issued a recall order for two products, and strongly suggested that Snow Brand voluntarily recall other products. The company dug in its heels until the city officials pressed the point. Then Snow Brand reluctantly agreed to the recall, on the condition that the company could be seen to be doing it voluntarily. But this didn't happen. In the event, the health authority publicized both the recall and the request.

In addition, Snow Brand is also believed to have withheld information about the exact nature of the incident. In what must have been a moment of desperation, Snow Brand initially claimed that the device where the contamination was found was used rarely. In fact it transpired it was used almost every day. The company also claimed that the area of contamination was 'about the size of a small coin' – but subsequent examination found it to be much bigger than that. The public perception – fuelled by the media coverage – was that the food poisoning was an inevitable result of a company suffocating itself with corporate arrogance.

To gain a flavour of the media coverage, it is worth looking at how the *Japan Times* reported the news that even more products were being recalled (this article appeared on the front page):

Japan's Snow Brand milk recalls more products as scandal widens

The tainted milk scandal at Japan's biggest dairy goods maker Snow Brand Milk Products Co escalated last Thursday as the company recalled products made by a plant not previously linked directly to the incident.

A company spokeswoman said some 125,000 packages of milk and dairy products made by a plant in central Japan were found to contain powdered skimmed milk that had been produced at a northern Japan facility plagued by a bacteria scare.

The recall comes after more than 14,800 people, mostly in the Osaka area in western Japan, fell ill in late June after drinking Snow Brand milk in one of Japan's most widespread food poisoning outbreaks.

The company said it had not received any complaints relating to the yoghurt, flavoured milk and other dairy products targeted by the latest recall, adding that 95,000 of the packages would no longer be on store shelves because they had passed their permissible sale date.

The northern Japan plant at the centre of the scandal was shut by Snow Brand on Sunday and ordered to remain closed indefinitely by local health authorities, after a toxin from staphylococcus aureus bacteria was found in preserved samples of the plant's powdered skimmed milk made in April.

A spokesman said on Wednesday the bacteria may have entered the milk as a result of a three-hour power failure on March 31 which left raw milk standing in high temperatures.

Some of that milk made its way into products at a plant in Osaka that was the source of the mass food-poisoning.

Snow Brand's shares were hit hard by the scandal, falling nearly 40 per cent. They have since recovered modestly and on Thursday ended up 0.23 per cent on the day at 427 yen.

Last Wednesday, the company said it posted a parent net loss of 11.2 billion yen for the April–July period due to the scandal, which forced it to temporarily close all 21 of its milk-producing plants in Japan.

As a result of the incident, sales for the company took a nosedive and Snow Brand's president, Tetsuro Ishikawa, closed eight of his factories.

Before the food poisoning, Snow Brand had a market share of 45 percent. This dropped to under 10 percent and the brand has still to recover back to its pre-2000 levels. The incident also took a personal toll for Tetsuro Ishikawa, who had to be admitted to hospital as a result of stress. Later he resigned and apologised to the media.

Lessons from Snow Brand

- *Respond quickly.* Snow Brand's initial response to the crisis was too slow as the company was reluctant to issue a full product recall and to communicate with the press.
- *Don't sound selfish.* When Snow Brand eventually did talk to the media, it focused on the financial consequences for the company, rather than the suffering of its food-poisoned customers.
- *Be prepared.* The company was ill-prepared when it made public statements and did not have all the information.

45 Rely tampons

Procter & Gamble's toxic shock

In 1980, Procter & Gamble launched a super-absorbent tampon called Rely. However, the super-absorbency of the product was a result of a synthetic substance called carboxymethyl cellulose, which would sometimes leave a synthetic residue inside a woman's body after the tampon had been removed. 'From the moment super-absorbent tampons hit the market there were published accounts of vaginal ulcerations, lesions, and lacerations,' writes Laurie Garrett in her 1994 book, *The Coming Plague*.

However, things became even more worrying later in the year with a sudden increase in cases of toxic shock syndrome in the state of Wisconsin. Almost all the cases were menstruating females. Following further research by health authorities it emerged that most victims had been using the Rely tampon.

This was clearly very bad news, not only for the victims, but also for Procter & Gamble, the company which had virtually started the tampon category in 1936. Furthermore, Rely had been one of the most expensive products ever to develop, with more than 20 years of research and marketing efforts behind it.

From the start of the crisis, Procter & Gamble acted defensively. When the Centers for Disease Control (CDC) in Atlanta started to investigate the link between Rely and toxic shock syndrome, Procter & Gamble began their own investigation which (surprise surprise) found no link. When the CDC published their findings, the link was backed up with comprehensive figures.

But Procter & Gamble dismissed this research as 'insufficient data in the hands of a bureaucracy.'

However, by this time the company had started to realize it was fighting a losing battle and began to co-operate and look for a compromise solution. Procter & Gamble suggested a warning label be added to the product. But when the results of the CDC study were confirmed by an independent research firm, Procter & Gamble had little choice but to suspend sales of the product.

The withdrawal of Rely from the market was estimated to cost US $75 million. However, although Procter & Gamble initially made matters worse by denying responsibility, the company was now embarked on a damage limitation exercise.

It worked jointly with the CDC to draft a consent agreement. The CDC allowed Procter & Gamble to deny any product defect or violation of federal law. In return Procter & Gamble promised to buy back any unused product and offered its scientific expertise to research the problem. The company also mounted a large-scale educational campaign.

In an article for the *Canadian Journal of Communication*, Drexel University's Priscilla Murphy explored Procter & Gamble's handling of the Rely tampon incident in relation to 'games theory'. She argued that by the end, Procter & Gamble's game plan had improved greatly:

> The latter stages of Procter & Gamble's strategy exemplify a wholly different approach to conflict. What had begun as a classic escalation game became a bargaining venture in which everyone's desires were examined and coordinated so that each player could live with the agreement. When we are talking about bargaining games we are really looking at the ways in which both sides in a conflict gradually come to agree on a single version of events, a single perspective. What resulted was a stable equilibrium point that, though not ideal, represented the best outcome for each side given the pressures from the other side.

So although the incidents of toxic shock syndrome spelt the end of the Rely brand, Procter & Gamble itself suffered small lasting damage and continues to produce some of the world's most popular tampon products.

Lessons from Rely

- *Co-operate don't aggravate*. If Procter & Gamble had co-operated with the health authorities from the start it would have been able to limit the negative media coverage.
- *Kill the brand, save the company*. For companies with numerous brands it is often better to admit defeat early on and terminate a brand for the sake of the overall reputation of the company.

46 Gerber's PR blunder

In 1986, Gerber, the German baby food manufacturer, made a critical PR mistake. When incidents of glass shards were found in its jars of baby food, Gerber remained tight-lipped and failed to issue a recall. This decision invited a lot of criticism with articles in *Business Week, Newsweek* and *Time* openly attacking the company on ethical grounds. Although the pieces of glass had not caused any fatalities, some babies had been severely hurt.

Glass fragments had originally been found in some Gerber products – namely, their apple-plum and apple-cherry juices – in 1984. But in that instance, Gerber handled the problem effectively. Although neither the company nor the authorities found a manufacturing-related cause, Gerber recalled over half a million jars of juice.

In 1986, however, there were over 200 reports of glass being found in Gerber's baby products across the United States. Although the authorities failed to discover anything that would warrant a recall, Maryland officials banned certain Gerber ranges from being sold anywhere in the state. Gerber's response? The company sued the state of Maryland. Other than this legal reaction, Gerber did nothing. Not a word was said to the media about the issue, in the hope that the whole fiasco would just pass by.

From Gerber's perspective, the company was doing nothing wrong. After all, nothing suggested that the fragments of glass were the fault of Gerber's manufacturing process. It had certainly been under no obligation to recall its products. The company therefore believed that the state of Maryland was in the wrong and took what it saw as the appropriate legal action.

As Gerber saw it, a recall would only serve to generate more media attention and would have a negative impact on sales. It would also be expensive to implement. But Gerber forgot one important thing. Brands are about the public's perception. It is not about proving who is right or who is wrong. By refusing to talk, Gerber was acting as though it had something to hide.

For a company that built its whole brand identity around the high quality and safety of its products, this was clearly a bad move. If you produce baby food, you have to constantly remind the public that you have parents' and babies' best interests at heart. By taking the state of Maryland to court, failing to issue a recall, and by then remaining silent, this was not the message Gerber put across.

Although Gerber's brands survived the crisis, most analysts now agree the incidents were not well managed and that Gerber's reputation suffered as a result.

Lessons from Gerber's PR blunder

- *Make a public response to a crisis.* As soon as the news arrived that some products had been tampered with, Gerber should have responded publicly and confirmed that it had the babies' best interests at heart. After that, it should have been open to all lines of media enquiry. Most of all, Gerber should have looked like it was doing something, such as coming up with new types of product packaging to prevent tampering.
- *Provide information.* At the time of the crisis, parents wanted information. For instance, Gerber could have told them how to distinguish between products that had been tampered with and those that had not.
- *Act tough.* In a paper on the ethical issues surrounding the glass scare, Dr Philip Rothschild recommended that Gerber should actively and publicly lobby for increased penalties for product tampering. 'They should make every effort to make someone else the bad guy,' he suggested.

47 RJ Reynolds' Joe Camel campaign

RJ Reynolds' attempt to create smokeless cigarettes (see Chapter 3) was not the tobacco company's only brand failure. In the 1990s, RJR got into big trouble over one of its campaigns to promote its leading brand of cigarettes, Camel. The campaign featured a character called Joe Camel, a cartoon camel who wore trendy clothes and sunglasses and who had a cigarette dangling from his mouth.

In 1991 the company was publicly charged in the *Journal of the American Medical Association* with targeting children through the Joe Camel character. That same year, the company got into further trouble when Janet Mangini, a San Francisco family lawyer, filed a lawsuit against the company. In doing this, she became the first person to legally challenge the tobacco industry for targeting children with its advertising.

However, the Joe Camel campaign survived until 1997, when various Californian local authorities intervened and came to Janet Mangini's aid. A trial date was set for December 1997. In preparation for the trial, the prosecuting lawyers discovered that RJR had researched the reasons why people start smoking and the smoking patterns of children. The lawsuit charged that as a result of this secret research, the tobacco giant developed advertising and promotional campaigns aimed directly at children, encouraging them to smoke Camel cigarettes.

As the trial approached, RJR asked whether the Mangini lawsuit could be resolved 'if the campaign was pulled.' However, in order to avoid court, RJR also had to make sure that the previously confidential internal documents regarding youth marketing and the Joe Camel campaign were made public. When the settlement was resolved, RJR stated that the 'Mangini action [. . .] was an early significant and unique driver of the overall legal and social controversy regarding underage smoking that led to the decision to phase out the Joe Camel campaign.'

However, as the RJR documents are still available on the Web, the negative PR damage has been a little more difficult to erase. As Stanton Glantz of UCSF University, which manages the online resource where the documents are kept, points out, 'the RJR information is very easy for the public to address. In contrast to recent releases of documents by the tobacco industry and the House Commerce Committee on the web, the Mangini documents are in a form that facilitates downloading them and understanding what they mean.'

In other words, this time the unpleasant taste wasn't left by the cigarette itself.

Lesson from Joe Camel

- *Youth marketing is a sensitive area.* Obviously any cigarette or alcohol manufacturer caught trying to push its product to children is in breach of the law. However, *all* companies need to tread carefully when it comes to youth marketing. For instance, in the UK brands such as Walkers and Tesco's have come under fire for trying to push their brand names through school-based campaigns. Also, it is important to remember that just because children have an interest in something, it doesn't mean that this is the way to reach them. For example, just because many children are interested in the occult (over 50 per cent according to one MORI poll), it clearly doesn't mean that marketers should fuel this interest.

48 Firestone tyres

The success of many brands is determined by the right partnership. This is certainly the case where one product is dependent on another. For instance, software developers and computer manufacturers need each other, and can often achieve better results if they join forces. Similarly, if you produce tyres you need to build and sustain good relations with a car company.

Any tyre manufacturer who can boast Ford Motor Company as a customer is therefore at a significant advantage. Equally, to *lose* such a customer could be viewed as disastrous and something which should be prevented at all costs, especially if you have been working together for almost a century. And yet on 21st May 2001, US tyre company Firestone announced that it would no longer supply Ford with original equipment tyres in either North or South America. Although Firestone was still prepared to work with Ford in Europe and Asia, this accounts for a meagre 25 per cent of its turnover with Ford. Even though three-quarters of tyres sold are 'aftermarket sales', a significant number of Ford customers replace their tyres with the same brand.

To appreciate the true significance of this wilful departure it is necessary to understand the two company's shared history. The relationship between Ford and Firestone certainly goes back a long way – to 1908 in fact, the year Harvey Firestone first supplied tyres to Henry Ford for the Model T. Although the two men had their disagreements, the Ford Motor Company used more of Firestone's tyres than any other brand, and the relationship survived long after the founders' deaths.

Even when the Japanese tyre company Bridgestone purchased Firestone in 1988, Ford continued to be its number one customer. In the 1990s, Ford was buying about 40 per cent of its tyres from Firestone, far more than from any other manufacturer.

However, Firestone has suffered more than any of its competitors from a number of high profile tyre failures. In 1977, the US government forced a recall of around 14 million tyres after 41 deaths and even more injuries were apparently caused by blowouts of the Firestone '500' tyres. Following all the negative PR this caused, Firestone lost its number one market position, to rival Goodyear.

Despite a decline in sales, the relationship with Ford was maintained intact. It was only when the quality of Firestone tyres was again placed under the spotlight in the late 1990s that trouble erupted between the two companies. In 1999, Ford received a number of complaints from customers in Thailand and Saudi Arabia, and ordered a recall of its cars in those regions. The company also asked Firestone to investigate these complaints. After taking six months to conduct the investigation, Firestone declared there was no problem with its tyres.

Now, however, the situation had spread to the United States, where a series of traffic accidents had prompted a Texan TV station to carry out an exposé of the problem. At the same time, the National Highway Traffic Safety Administration (NHTSA) launched an official enquiry in which both Ford and Firestone had to submit evidence.

While Firestone agreed to co-operate with the NHTSA, at first the company refused to supply any information on faulty tyres to Ford. When it eventually did so, Ford immediately subjected the data to heavy scrutiny and showed its findings to the NHTSA. The findings apparently confirmed that the tread of the tyres separated when the car was driven at high speed. Within four days, the NHTSA issued a mandatory recall notice.

Firestone was still determined to fight its corner. When Ford suggested the company publish all the data on its tyres, Firestone refused, maintaining that the main cause of the accidents was the design and specification of the Ford Explorer. Their argument is explained by the editorial team of the just-auto.com Web site:

In order to give a more comfortable ride, Ford had ignored Firestone's recommendation of tyre pressures in the 30–36 psi range and had recommended pressures at the bottom end of that range. Any neglect by owners had resulted in under-inflated tyres which ran hotter than they should, especially in desert conditions, and if the treads did strip off, the vehicles were more inclined to roll over because they have a higher centre of gravity.

Whether Firestone has a point or not, its brand has been considerably damaged by the very public mud-slinging as both it and Ford tried to dodge the blame for the accidents. It all came to a head when Ford announced it would replace up to 13 million Firestone tyres. Ford explained that, 'tyres not covered in the original recall could experience increased failure rates.' This decision came a day after Firestone abandoned Ford as a customer.

As the investigations of more than 100 deaths in tyre-related crashes of Ford Explorers continued, Firestone was rapidly losing the public's confidence. In one *Fortune* magazine survey, the company dropped to the bottom of a chart of most-admired companies.

'Looking at the brand today, I would say it's a highly challenged brand,' says Gwen Morrison, a branding analyst at Chicago-based marketing agency Frankel. 'The very core of what tyre brands have stood for is safety. You see ads with a baby sitting in a stack of tyres; there had been a halo over the entire industry.'

The fact that Ford and Firestone failed to provide clear, consistent and comprehensive information to the public, explaining the crashes, was an obvious mistake. Sure, however they would have been handled, the crashes were always going to be bad news. But by sitting on information and failing to co-operate, Firestone has put its own long-term future under greater threat than it would have been otherwise.

Many branding experts now expect parent company Bridgestone to abandon the Firestone brand altogether, and concentrate on its own branded tyres instead.

Lessons from Firestone

- *Be honest with customers.* The tyre failures themselves have probably caused less damage than evidence that Firestone held back information about the problems.
- *Act fast.* In the event of a brand crisis, such as a product recall, companies need to act fast to re-establish customer confidence. Waiting six months before publishing your findings is only going to fuel negative speculation.

- *Be sensitive.* By squabbling with Ford instead of offering sympathy to the car-crash victims, Firestone appeared insensitive.
- *Cover worst-case scenarios with business partners.* Partnerships built for the long term must include mutually agreed-upon responsibilities and communication plans, recommends Robert Desisto, brand analyst at Gartner Research. 'More specifically, these partnerships must include a method of listening to customer complaints through one another's customer support centres, as well as a method of sharing technical support data earlier to prevent lost sales as well as the loss of the more intangible customer goodwill,' he says.
- *Be aware that prediction equals protection.* Owing to the fact that customers were complaining about the tyre failures years before the accidents made international headlines, Firestone should have been able to predict the problem and resolve it in advance.
- *Remember that perception is everything.* Whatever the truth behind why the tyres split, the poor handling of the issue by Firestone meant that the brand came under fire. If you look as though you are hiding relevant information from the public, the perception will be negative, regardless of the truth.
- *Keep hold of your key brand asset.* Firestone's marketing efforts had always been designed to instil the notion of 'safety' into the public's mind. When it lost this key brand asset through all the hostile publicity, Firestone was in big trouble.

49 Farley's infant milk

The salmonella incident

When the UK Central Public Health Laboratory made the connection between Farley's infant milk and salmonella in 1985, the story made the headlines. The product was recalled immediately at a cost of £8 million. Farley's parent company Glaxo Smith-Kline was forced to put Farley's into liquidation and sold its two plants to high-street chemist Boots for £18 million.

Boots had an almost impossible task in rebuilding the brand, given the amount of negative media coverage it had suffered. After all, health scares are always damaging for brands, but health scares involving babies are, if anything, even more catastrophic.

Furthermore, while Farley's had been off the shelves, its two main competitors – Cow & Gate and Wyeth – had stepped up their production leaving little room for Farley's to squeeze back in. Although Boots ploughed millions into promoting and marketing Farley, the brand's market share was never able to return to the levels it had reached before the salmonella incident. After years of persistence, eventually Boots sold the business to Heinz in 1994.

Lessons from Farley's

- *Keep a look out for internal threats.* The salmonella incident had been avoidable because it had been caused by an employee not following adequate procedures.

- *Remember that competitors will take advantage.* After Farley's products had been taken off the shelves, its main competitors seized the opportunity and made it harder for Farley's to make a comeback.

CHAPTER 6

Culture failures

Brands operate on a global scale. Brand names such as Nike, Coca-Cola, McDonald's, Gillette, Adidas, Disney, Marlboro, Sony, Budweiser, Microsoft and Pepsi are now recognized across the world. The dismantling of trade barriers, combined with the rise of global communications technologies such as the Internet, has meant that companies can expand into new markets faster than ever before.

However, many companies have confused the era of globalization with an era of homogenization. If they have had success with one product in one market they have assumed they can have equal success in another. All they believe they have to do is set up a Web site in the relevant language, run an ad campaign and set up a similar distribution network. What they forget to understand is that there is more to a country than its language, currency or gross domestic product. The cultural differences between, and often within, countries can greatly affect the chances of success for a brand.

In order to succeed, brands must cater for the specific tastes of each market they enter. If these tastes change, then the brand must change also. As the bumpy ride experienced by Kellogg's in India (the first example included in this chapter) indicates, companies which fail to accommodate and acknowledge these vast cultural differences face a long battle in replicating their success at home in other markets.

However, understanding cultural differences is not just about international markets. It is also about understanding the specific culture of the brand. When companies acquire a brand that wasn't theirs to begin with, they can often make similar *faux pas* as when they move into a foreign market. However, instead of making the mistake of misinterpreting the market they misinterpret the brand. This happened when CBS acquired the guitar company Fender and when Quaker Oats bought the soft drink Snapple. Although the companies spent millions on marketing, they lost market share as they didn't understand exactly where the market was, and what the customer wanted. As a result, in both cases, the acquisition weakened the brand.

50 Kellogg's in India

Kellogg's is, of course, a mighty brand. Its cereals have been consumed around the globe more than any of its rivals. Sub-brands such as Corn Flakes, Frosties and Rice Krispies are the breakfast favourites of millions.

In the late 1980s, the company had reached an all-time peak, commanding a staggering 40 per cent of the US ready-to-eat market from its cereal products alone. By that time, Kellogg's had over 20 plants in 18 countries world wide, with yearly sales reaching above US $6 billion.

However, in the 1990s Kellogg's began to struggle. Competition was getting tougher as its nearest rivals General Mills increased the pressure with its Cheerios brand. Kellogg's management team was accused of being 'unimaginative', and of 'spoiling some of the world's top brands' in a 1997 article in *Fortune* magazine.

In core markets such as the United States and the UK, the cereal industry has been stagnant for over a decade, as there has been little room for growth. Therefore, from the beginning of the 1990s Kellogg's looked beyond its traditional markets in Europe and the United States in search of more cereal-eating consumers. It didn't take the company too long to decide that India was a suitable target for Kellogg's products. After all, here was a country with over 950 million inhabitants, 250 million of whom were middle class, and a completely untapped market potential.

In 1994, three years after the barriers to international trade had opened in India, Kellogg's decided to invest US $65 million into launching its number one brand, Corn Flakes. The news was greeted optimistically by Indian economic experts such as Bhagirat B Merchant, who in 1994 was the director of the Bombay Stock Exchange. 'Even if Kellogg's has only a two percent market share, at 18 million consumers they will have a larger market than in the US itself,' he said at the time.

However, the Indian sub-continent found the whole concept of eating breakfast cereal a new one. Indeed, the most common way to start the day in India was with a bowl of hot vegetables. While this meant that Kellogg's had few direct competitors it also meant that the company had to promote not only its product, but also the very idea of eating breakfast cereal in the first place.

The first sales figures were encouraging, and indicated that breakfast cereal consumption was on the rise. However, it soon became apparent that many people had bought Corn Flakes as a one-off, novelty purchase. Even if they liked the taste, the product was too expensive. A 500-gram box of Corn Flakes cost a third more than its nearest competitor. However, Kellogg's remained unwilling to bow to price pressure and decided to launch other products in India, without doing any further research of the market. Over the next few years Indian cereal buyers were introduced to Kellogg's Wheat Flakes, Frosties, Rice Flakes, Honey Crunch, All Bran, Special K and Chocos Chocolate Puffs – none of which have managed to replicate the success they have encountered in the West.

Furthermore, the company's attempts to 'Indianize' its range have been disastrous. Its Mazza-branded series of fusion cereals, with flavours such as mango, coconut and rose, failed to make a lasting impression.

Acknowledging the relative failure of these brands in India, Kellogg's has come up with a new strategy to establish the company's brand equity in the market. If it can't sell cereal, it's going to try and sell biscuits. The news of this brand extension was covered in depth in the *Indian Express* newspaper in 2000:

The company has been looking at alternate product categories to counter poor off take for its breakfast cereal brands in the Indian market, say sources. Meanwhile, the Kellogg main stay – breakfast cereals – has seen frenzied marketing activity from the company's end. The idea behind the effort is to establish the Kellogg brand equity in the market.

'The company is concentrating on establishing its brand name in the market irrespective of the off take. The focus is entirely on being present and visible on the retail shelves with a wide range of products,' explains a company dealer in Mumbia.

As per the trade, Kellogg India has disclosed to the dealers its intention of launching more than one new product onto the market every month for the next six months.

These rapid-fire launches were supported with extensive 'below-the-line' activity, such as consumer offers on half of Kellogg's cereal boxes. Although most of the biscuit ranges have so far been a success with children, due in part to their low price, Kellogg's is still struggling in the cereal category.

Although the company tried to be more sensitive to the requirements of the market, through subtle taste alterations, the high price of the cereals remains a deterrent. According to a study conducted by research firm PROMAR International, titled 'The Sub-Continent in Transition: A strategic assessment of food, beverage, and agribusiness opportunities in India in 2010,' the price factor will restrict Kellogg's from further market growth. 'While Kellogg's has ushered in a shift in Indian breakfast habits and adapted its line of cereal flavours to meet the Indian palate, the price of the product still restricts consumption to urban centres and affluent households,' the study reports.

Kellogg's tough ride in India has not been unique. Here are some further examples of brands which have managed to misjudge the market:

- *Mercedes-Benz*. In 1995 the German car giant opened a plant in India to produce its E-class Sedan. The car, which was targeted at the growing ranks of India's wealthy middle class, failed to inspire. By 1997, the plant was using only 10 per cent of its 20,000 car capacity. 'Indians turned up their noses at the Sedan – a model older than those sold in Europe,' reported *Business Week* at the time. 'Now Mercedes has to reassess its mistakes and start exporting excess cars to Africa and elsewhere.'
- *Lufthansa*. Germany's Lufthansa airline joined forces with Indian company, the Modi Group, to launch a new domestic private airline, Modi-Luft, in 1993. However, three years later ModiLuft had gone bust and Lufthansa filed a lawsuit against one of the Modi brothers, claiming he had used funds obtained from the German company in other ventures. In return, the Modi Group accused Lufthansa of charging too much and of producing defective planes.

- *Coca-Cola.* The Coca-Cola company understood that distribution was the key to building a strong Indian brand. It therefore decided to buy out one of India's most successful soft drink companies and manufacturers of popular soda brand Thums Up. However, although this gave Coca-Cola an instant distribution network, Thums Up remained more popular than Coke for many years. Most Indians initially thought that the new entry to the market wasn't fizzy enough.

- *Whirlpool.* When Whirlpool launched its refrigerators on the Indian market, it found the market unwilling to buy larger sizes than the standard 165 litres.

- *MTV.* When MTV India was launched, the aim was to bring Western rock, rap and pop to the sub-continent. Now, however, the music policy has shifted to accommodate Indian genres such as bhangra.

- *Domino's Pizza.* Initially, Domino's Pizza transferred its Western offerings direct to the Indian market, but the company eventually realized that it had to bow to local tastes, as Arvind Nair, chief executive officer at Domino's Pizza India explains. 'Initially, our focus was to stay only in metropolitan areas, but in the last two years we have felt the need to spread ourselves into "mini metros" and B-category towns. We have also experimented with our taste options, especially when we went into smaller towns. We have focused on more regional flavours now,' he says. As a result of this change of strategy, Domino's came up with localized toppings such as 'Peppy Paneer' and 'Chicken Chettinad'. This move was greeted with a wry smile from Domino's main Indian competitor, US Pizza, which was the first to offer local topping. 'In 1995, when we offered tandoori chicken and paneer toppings, some made fun of us saying, why not offer spaghetti and pasta toppings? The same companies are now offering chole and spicy masala pizzas,' says Wahid Berenjian, the managing director for US Pizza. He told the Hindu newspaper *Business Line* that US brands such as Domino's made the mistake of thinking that US tastes are universal. 'You cannot change the taste buds that were developed more than a thousand years ago,' he said.

- *Citibank.* When Citibank entered the Indian market, the firm's aim was to target only high-income earners. But, in the words of the *Business Line* newspaper, Citibank soon realized that 'in India it makes sense to go the mass banking way rather than the class banking way.'

One of the reasons why Kellogg's and these other brands' passage to India was not smooth was because they had been blinded by figures. The Indian population may be verging on 1 billion, but its middle class accounts for only a quarter of that figure. However, a 1996 survey conducted by the Indian National Council on Applied Economic Research in Delhi found that the sub-continent's 'consumer class' numbers are around 100 million people at the most, and that buying habits and tastes vary greatly between the Indian regions. After all, India has 17 official languages and six major religions spread throughout 25 states.

As a result, only those companies which are in tune with India's many cultural complexities can stand a chance. One of the companies which has managed to get it right is Unilever. However, the conglomerate has had a head start on those Western companies which entered the market after 1991. Indeed, Unilever's soap and toothpaste products have been available in India since 1887, when the sub-continent was still the crown jewel of the British Empire. The secret to Unilever's longevity in India is distribution. Hindustan Lever Limited (Unilever's Indian arm) has products available in a staggering total of 10 million small shops throughout rural India.

As for Kellogg's, it remains to be seen whether its move into other product categories, such as snack food, will be able to help strengthen its brand. The dilemma that it may face is that if it becomes associated with biscuits rather than cereals, core products like Corn Flakes could become a marginal part of the company's brand identity in India.

'Kellogg's is caught in a bind,' one Indian brand analyst remarked in India's *Business Line* newspaper. 'It realises that cornflakes can make money only in the long haul, so it needs a product which will give it some accelerated growth and the tonnage it is desperately looking for. However, its area of strength worldwide lies in breakfast cereal and not in the snack food category.'

However, other impartial Indian commentators are more optimistic about Kellogg's future prospects within the sub-continent. Among those who believe Kellogg's will eventually succeed is Jagdeep Kapoor, the managing director of Indian marketing firm Samiska Marketing Consultants. 'With every product offering, Kellogg's chances improve based on its learning in the Indian market,' he says.

Only time will tell.

Lessons from Kellogg's

- *Do your homework.* Why did Kellogg's cereals have a tough ride in India? 'It was just clumsy cultural homework,' says Titoo Ahluwalia, chairman of market research company ORG MARG in Bombay.
- *Don't underestimate local competitors.* Although Indian brands were worried they would struggle against a new wave of foreign competition following the market opening of 1991, they were wrong. 'Multinational corporations must not start with the assumption that India is a barren field,' said C K Prahalad, business professor at the University of Michigan, in a *Business Week* article. 'The trick is not to be too big.'
- *Remember that square pegs don't fit into round holes.* When Kellogg's first launched Corn Flakes in India it was essentially launching a Western product attempting to appeal to Indian tastes. Globalization may be an increasing trend, but regional identities, customs and tastes are as distinct as ever. It may be easy for brand managers of global brands to view the world as homogenous, where consumer demands are all the same, but the reality is rather different. 'There is a bigger opportunity in localizing your offerings and the smarter companies are realizing this,' says Ramanujan Sridhar, chief executive officer at Indian marketing and advertising consultancy firm Brand Comm.
- *Don't try and make consumers strangers to their culture.* 'The rules are very clear,' says Wahid Berenjian, the managing director for US Pizza (which has successfully launched a range of pizzas with Indian toppings) in an article for the Hindu newspaper, *Business Line*. 'You can alienate me a bit from my culture, but you cannot make me a stranger to my culture. The society is much stronger than any company or product.' Brands who want to succeed in India and other culturally distinct markets need to remember this.

51 Hallmark in France

Hallmark greeting cards have proven immensely popular in both the UK and the United States. Catering for every special occasion – from birthdays to weddings and from Mother's Day to passing your driving test – the cards are sent by thousands of people every single day of the year.

The signature (or 'hallmark') of Hallmark cards is the 'special message'. The advantage of buying from Hallmark is that you don't have to think about what to write – it is usually all written for you. 'Thank you for being such a special daughter.' 'These birthday wishes are especially for you,' and so on, normally followed by a rather sentimental poem inside.

While this formula may be successful in many countries, it has not proved universal. For instance, when Hallmark tried to introduce their cards in France, no-one bought them as people preferred to write in the cards themselves. Furthermore, the syrupy sentiment inherent within the pre-printed messages did not appeal to the Gallic taste. After a few months Hallmark admitted defeat and withdrew its brand.

Lesson from Hallmark

- *Brands need to acknowledge cultural differences*. Very few brands have been able to be transferred into different cultures without changes to their formula. Even Coca-Cola and McDonald's vary their products for different markets.

Translation troubles

Often the problems inherent in international markets relate to translation trouble. The language of commerce may be one which everyone understands, but many businesses have made massive branding mistakes when trying to replicate the success of their advertising campaigns in markets where their native tongue isn't spoken.

Outlined below are just some of the biggest *faux pas* that have occurred through international marketing.

52 Pepsi in Taiwan

In order to keep a singular identity throughout the world, many companies stick with the same marketing campaign and brand message in every country. However, this occasionally creates difficulties. For instance, in Taiwan Pepsi's advertising slogan 'Come alive with the Pepsi generation' was translated as 'Pepsi will bring your ancestors back from the dead.'

53 Schweppes Tonic Water in Italy

In Italy, a promotional campaign for Schweppes Tonic Water failed when the product name was translated as 'Schweppes Toilet Water'. Subsequent campaigns have had better results.

54 Chevy Nova and others

Of all products, cars have had the most translation problems. When people chuckled at General Motors' Chevy Nova in Latin America, the automotive giant was perplexed. Until, that is, someone pointed out that 'Nova' means 'It doesn't go' in Spanish. Then there was the Mitsubishi Pajero sport utility that caused embarrassment in Spain, where 'pajero' is slang for 'masturbator'. Toyota's Fiera car proved controversial in Puerto Rico, where 'fiera' translates to 'ugly old woman'. Likewise few Germans were enthusiastic about owning Rolls-Royce's 'Silver Animal Droppings' car. To the English speaking world it bears the more romantic name 'Silver Mist'. And finally, Ford didn't have the reception they expected in Brazil when their 'Pinto' car flopped. Then they discovered that in Brazilian Portuguese slang, 'pinto' means 'small penis'.

55 Electrolux in the United States

Scandinavian vacuum manufacturer Electrolux raised a few eyebrows in the United States when it came up with the slogan 'Nothing sucks like an Electrolux'. It later reworked its strap line.

56 Gerber in Africa

When baby food manufacturer Gerber started to sell its products in Africa it used the same packaging as for Western markets. This packaging included a picture of a baby boy on the label. Surprised at low sales, Gerber discovered that in Africa, as most customers can't read English, Western companies generally put pictures on the label of what's inside.

57 Coors in Spain

Coors beer had equally bad luck in Spain with its 'Turn it loose' slogan. It translated as 'You will suffer from diarrhoea'.

58 Frank Perdue's chicken in Spain

Sticking with Spain, US food brand Frank Perdue's chicken campaign created confusion with the strap line 'It takes a strong man to make a tender chicken.' In Spain this became 'It takes an aroused man to make a chicken affectionate.'

59 Clairol's Mist Stick in Germany

When Clairol launched its 'Mist Stick' curling iron in Germany, the company apparently had no idea that 'Mist' was a slang term for manure. The company discovered that few women were crying out for a manure stick.

60 Parker Pens in Mexico

Parker Pens alarmed its Mexican market with ads intended to read 'It won't leak in your pocket and embarrass you' because, in fact, the ad stated 'It won't leak in your pocket and impregnate you.' The company had managed to confuse 'embarrass' with the Spanish verb 'embrazar' or 'to impregnate'.

61 American Airlines in Mexico

When American Airlines decided to advertise the luxurious aspect of flying business class to their Mexican customers, they thought it would make sense to focus on the leather seats. They therefore used the slogan 'fly in leather' which, in Spanish, read 'Vuelo en Cuero'. What the Spanish dictionary had neglected to inform them was that the phrase 'en cuero' is a slang term for 'in the nude'. It soon emerged that there was little demand for mile-high naturism among Mexico's business flyers.

62 Vicks in Germany

Vapour-rub manufacturer Vicks failed to attract much custom for its products in Germany. The problem was that 'V' is pronounced as an 'F' in German, meaning Vicks sounds like the German equivalent of the 'f' word.

63 Kentucky Fried Chicken in Hong Kong

KFC's 'finger lickin' good' slogan is used the world over to highlight the tastiness of the product. However, when the phrase was translated into Chinese for the Hong Kong market, it came out as 'eat your fingers off'. Needless to say, most customers opted for the fries instead.

64 CBS Fender

A tale of two cultures

For guitar fans, the Fender brand is an icon. Fender guitars, such as the Stratocaster and the Telecaster, were associated with the rock and roll scene of the 1950s and were later played by many of the most famous rock musicians. John Lennon and George Harrison both owned Stratocasters, and Jimi Hendrix also helped to turn that particular model of electric guitar into a legend.

However, at some point in the early 1960s Leo Fender made the near-fatal decision to sell his company. In 1965 he found a buyer in the form of CBS, which already at that time was one of the largest players in the music business, with its record labels and radio shows proving extremely popular and successful. The deal was viewed by both parties as a logical one. After all, CBS was in the music business and Fender made musical instruments. How was that for synergy?

Initially, the move seemed to be a success. As the electric guitar revolutionized rock music in the late 1960s and the 1970s, CBS-Fender remained the main manufacturer of the instrument. Eric Clapton, Mark Knopfler and almost any other guitar legend from that period played a Fender guitar.

By 1975, though, the company started to lose market share. 'The problem was, CBS didn't know all that much about real manufacturing,' says Morgan Ringwald, the current PR director for Fender Musical Instruments Corporation. 'After about ten years, they lost sight of all quality control, let their patents lapse, and forgot to keep putting money into research and development. Pretty soon, Asian manufacturers were able to make cheaper and better copies of Fender designs.'

The company's major selling point – the Stratocaster guitar – was neglected. According to the Fender lover's Web site, Fender-strat.com, this was a major mistake:

> The conglomerate eventually did what no-one else could: make the Strat less powerful. As time went by, new players bought from Fender while experienced players turned to vintage Strats for the eternal brilliance of its design, combined with the understated remarkable versatility [. . .] By 1985, the Strat had been copied, stripped, doctored and otherwise abused.

In 1981 CBS had recruited a new management team to 're-invent' the Fender brand. They put together a five-year business plan based on the idea of improving the quality of Fender products. However, the real turnaround didn't occur until 1985, when CBS decided to divest all of its non-broadcasting businesses. Fender was subsequently purchased by a group of employees and investors led by William Schultz.

The Fender company which emerged from this 're-birth' (as Fender fans like to call it) was certainly smaller than CBS-Fender had ever been. CBS sold only the Fender name patents, and the parts that were left over in stock. No buildings or machines had been involved in the deal. However, what the new Fender company did have was a team of employees who understood exactly what the Fender brand was all about. Indeed, many had been with the company since Leo Fender had begun making guitars and amplifiers back in the 1940s. It didn't take long for the brand to reclaim its place in the hearts of guitar fans worldwide.

During the 1990s, Fender's sales increased dramatically and the company extended its product offerings around the growing requirements of the electrical guitarists, producing not only strings and guitars, but also audio products such as amplifiers and mixing boards. The secret to Fender's continued success rests in its understanding of the values that made the brand so popular in the first place – namely, craftsmanship and a deep understanding of the contemporary guitarist. When those values were temporarily forgotten, during CBS' reign of 1965 to 1985, the brand suffered.

Now, Fender is back on track and its customers are more appreciative of the brand than ever before. As the Fender-strat.com Web site enthuses,

'Fender has maintained its hold on the hearts, minds, and fingers of guitarists everywhere with relentless quality, as well as some of the highest research and development commitments in the industry.'

This view is supported by another non-official guitar Web site, harmony-central.com. On that site, Fender-lover Richard Smith congratulates the brand on surviving the CBS years and on its return to its core values. 'The Fender company is still shaping the way the world plays and hears music, and making life better for guitar players,' he says.

Lessons from Fender

- *Understand your product.* One of the main problems CBS faced was that it had little real understanding of what exactly made Fender so special. 'Most companies don't do their homework,' says Howard Moskowitz, the president of New York-based market research firm, Moskowitz Jacobs. 'They don't really know anything about the dynamics of their product, about the drivers of liking in a product that they're going to go into.'
- *Focus on what built the brand.* CBS neglected the attention to quality and craftsmanship which had established the Fender brand in the first place.

65 Quaker Oats' Snapple

Failing to understand the essence of the brand

In 1994, food giant the Quaker Oats Company bought a quirky soft-drink brand called Snapple for US $1.7 billion. The company felt confident that the drink brand was worth the price tag, because they had already achieved an astounding success with the sports drink Gatorade.

However, in terms of brand identity the two drinks couldn't have been further apart. Gatorade was about sports and a high-energy, athletic image. Snapple, on the other hand, had always been promoted as a New Agey and fashionable alternative to standard soft drink brands.

As many commentators at the time observed, Quaker Oats simply didn't understand what the Snapple identity was all about. Specifically, there were two main reasons why Quaker's three years in charge of Snapple diminished the brand's value.

Reason number one has to do with distribution. Before 1994, most Snapple drinks were sold at small shops and petrol stations. However, Quaker deployed its usual mass marketing techniques and placed the brand in supermarkets and other inappropriate locations.

The other problem was the way Quaker decided to promote the product, abandoning eccentric advertising campaigns in favour of a more conservative approach. The day after Quaker announced that it would sell the Snapple drink business for US $300 million (over five times lower than the price they had bought it for), the *New York Times* pointed the finger at the misguided advertising campaigns. 'Quaker discontinued its quirky campaign featuring a Snapple employee named Wendy Kaufman, and replaced it with one in which Snapple boasted that it would be happy to be third behind Coca-Cola and Pepsi in the beverage market.' The 'real life' US advertising featuring Wendy Kaufman, a receptionist reading fan letters from consumers, had been a real hit, but Quaker decided to come up with a new advertising campaign using the same company which produced its Gatorade campaigns. The end result was a counterproductive advertising campaign which succeeded in 'normalizing' Snapple's previously quirky identity.

As sales started to slide, Quaker believed it held the solution – send sales reps out on to the streets to ask people to try the product for free. Then the company back-tracked on the new Snapple advertising strategy with artier ads more in tune with the brand's original identity. But it didn't work. Snapple was fast losing its innovative image, along with its customer base.

When Quaker sold Snapple to Michael Weinstein and his colleagues, the brand was in trouble:

> We inherited a brand in a deep sales slide, losing 20 percent annually, and a demoralized organization. At the time Snapple was six times the size of our company, but only two Snapple headquarters personnel from Chicago chose to join the new team in New York. Few outside observers believed a small beverage company competing with Coke and Pepsi and with a new team could turn Snapple around, but we outlined a strategy and vision of success that the entire organisation could rally around.

In an interview with *Fast Company* in 2001, Michael explained how his company, called Triarc, managed to undo the marketing and advertising failures which occurred under Quaker's ownership of the brand. 'We tried to create an atmosphere that was fun and timely,' he said. 'We introduced our first new product two weeks after we bought the company. That's fast.' Another part of the strategy was to bring back the adverts featuring Wendy the receptionist.

Gradually, Snapple's original customer returned and the brand again increased in value. In 2000, Cadbury Schweppes bought Snapple for US $1 billion and Michael Weinstein moved with the brand. He is currently the president of 'global innovation' at Cadbury, and Snapple is now fully restored after its rather rocky ride.

Lessons from Snapple

- *Accept that different brands need different distribution.* Quaker believed that Snapple could be pushed through Gatorade's distribution system. 'It turned out that Quaker's distribution competences could not be leveraged to push Snapple because the image of the two brands is very distinct,' says Sanjay Goel, an assistant professor at the Department of Management Studies at the University of Minnesota. Snapple's New Agey image had been supported by the fact it had been sold through thousands of small-sized and independent distributors, Quaker decided it was best to use supermarkets and other larger outlets.
- *Understand the brand.* Ultimately, Quaker failed to hold onto Snapple's brand value because it did not understand the essence of the brand identity.

CHAPTER 7

People failures

The people behind a brand are its main ambassadors. If those people fall out with each other, act illegally or make negative statements about their products, then a crisis may quickly develop. This is especially true in those cases where the people *are* the brand, as in the case of a pop group or a TV personality such as Martha Stewart or Rosie O'Donnell (both of whom have done much to diminish the value of their branded personalities in the United States). It is also true when people at the highest level of the company are caught acting irresponsibly.

The most obvious case of 'people failure' in recent times is that of the Enron scandal, where fraudulent activities were associated with individuals at the very top of the company. However, corruption is only an extreme and rather dramatic aspect of people failure.

Sometimes brands can die as a result of the words that come out of the chief executive's mouth. For instance, the Ratner's brand of jewellery lost its market value overnight when Gerald Ratner declared his products were 'crap'. Whether or not this was a fair assessment was beside the point, the very fact that he said it was enough to destroy the brand.

The real lesson is that no matter how much time, money and energy is poured into a brand or corporate strategy, it ultimately depends on the behaviour of individuals whether or not this strategy remains on track. The higher up the individual, the more he or she is seen as representative of the brand. To borrow a useful phrase from John Karolefski, former editor-in-chief of *Brand Marketing* magazine, 'the fish rots from the head.' In other words, those with the most responsibility must act the most responsibly. 'The CEO must buy into and be part of the strategy from its inception,' says Karolefski. 'The head of the company sets the tone throughout the entire organisation. He or she will also be the most likely spokesperson for the company and must be credible.'

Karolefski has also written lucidly about the Enron and related Arthur Andersen scandals. 'A critical element in these cases is that the crisis and the resulting damage did not come from a faulty product,' he told *Brand Marketing* readers. 'All of the faults, the problems, the improprieties, the theft, all came from within the corporation, and in many or most cases, from inside the executive suite or from the CEO directly.'

On the face of it, there may not be much in common between Enron and Planet Hollywood, or Arthur Andersen and the first reality TV pop group, but there is a unifying factor. In the case of Enron it was corruption, while in the case of Planet Hollywood it was a simple case of celebrity self-deception, but either way the brand ambassadors ultimately failed the brand.

66 Enron

Failing the truth

Little remains to be said about the rise and scandalous fall of Texan energy giant Enron. In the relatively short space of 15 years, Enron rose from nowhere to become the seventh largest company in the United States, and the most well-known energy supplier in the world. It boasted over 21,000 employees and had a presence in more than 40 countries.

As well as generating energy, the firm also generated a rather healthy brand identity. It won *Fortune* magazine's award for 'Most Innovative Company in America' six years running, and was also high in the rankings for the same magazine's 'Best Companies to Work For' chart. The company projected an image of being a good corporate citizen and published a social and environmental report which looked at the moves it was taking with regard to the environmental consequences of its business, its employee relations and (most ironically) its anti-corruption and bribery policies.

Over the years, Enron depicted itself as a highly profitable, growing company. Of course, in 2001–02 this turned out to be a lie – one of the biggest in corporate history. The company's profit statements were proved to be untrue, and it emerged that massive debts had been hidden so that they weren't evident in the company's accounts. Enron's accountancy firm, Arthur Andersen, was involved in the shredding of documents relating to Enron's accounts, which meant the impact of the scandal was going to be catastrophic for that firm's reputation as well. As the depth of the deception unfolded, investors and creditors retreated, forcing the firm into Chapter 11 bankruptcy in December 2001. When such facts came to light, Enron executives made matters worse by refusing to testify and arguing that they had no chance of a fair trial.

The Enron scandal also had political implications, because of the firm's close links with the White House. Enron ploughed millions of dollars into George Bush's 2000 election campaign. Although Bush was a personal friend of Enron CEO Kenneth Lay, he was quick to distance himself from any direct involvement with the firm.

The long-term effects of the scandal will be felt for years to come, and the Enron name is already beyond repair and forever likely to be synonymous with 'corporate irresponsibility.'

Lessons from Enron

- *Don't lie.* The whole company image portrayed by Enron proved to be a complete fraud. And as soon as one lie emerged, it didn't take too long before the rest were unravelled.
- *Be legal.* A rather obvious lesson, but one which is still being broken at every level of the corporate community.
- *Be open.* Enron managed to make a terrible situation even worse by refusing to acknowledge any wrongdoing after the facts emerged.

67 Arthur Andersen

Shredding a reputation

If the Enron scandal proved anything, it was the interconnected nature of the modern business world. After all, Enron had a lot of corporate connections, particularly in its home state of Texas. 'Within two or three degrees of separation, virtually everybody would have a connection to Enron,' said Richard Murray, director for the University of Houston's Centre for Public Policy.

However, while the Enron association has had a negative impact on the Texan corporate community, for those firms directly involved with Enron's day-to-day business practices, the result has been catastrophic. For Enron's accountancy firm, Arthur Andersen, the association has proved fatal.

After all, if it was about anything the Enron scandal was about accountancy. Specifically it was about shredding documents relating to Enron's accounts and concealing massive debts, a fact that immediately implied a considerable element of complicity on the part of the accountancy firm. This complicity was implied further when David Duncan, Enron's chief auditor at Andersen, appeared involuntarily at the first investigation into the scandal and then refused to speak in order to avoid incriminating himself. Even when Joseph Berardino, Andersen's chief executive, vigorously defended his firm's role in the affair, he was unable to undo the damage. Once it was found guilty of deliberately destroying evidence, the firm suffered severe brand damage and the tremors were felt throughout the entire accountancy industry.

Lessons from Arthur Andersen

- *Understand that businesses are interconnected.* No firm is completely immune from other businesses. Andersen and Enron's actions have been impossible to separate, at least in the mind of the public.
- *Don't send mixed messages.* As the plot thickened, different versions of events started to emerge from inside Andersen.

68 Ratner's

When honesty is not the best policy

One of the most popular and influential books ever written about marketing is *The 22 Immutable Laws of Marketing*, written by Al Ries and Jack Trout and first published in 1993. Their fifteenth 'law' is 'the law of candour'. This states that if a company admits a negative aspect about a brand, the consumer will think more highly about that brand because of the company's sheer honesty.

Ries and Trout say that it goes against corporate and human nature to acknowledge a problem or weakness. 'First and foremost,' they write, 'candour is very disarming. Every negative statement you make about yourself is instantly accepted as truth. Positive statements, on the other hand, are looked at as dubious at best. Especially in an advertisement.'

The authors go on to give a list of companies which have used this honest approach to great effect. They admire, for instance, the strap line 'Avis is only number two in rent-a-cars.' They also declare that 'positive thinking has been highly overrated':

The explosive growth of communications in our society has made people defensive and cautious about companies trying to sell them anything. Admitting a problem is something that very few companies do.

When a company starts a message by admitting a problem, people tend to almost instinctively open their minds. Think about the times that someone came to you with a problem and how quickly you got involved and wanted to help. Now think about people starting off a conversation about some wonderful things they are doing. You probably were a lot less interested.

Another example given is that of Listerine mouthwash, a brand that successfully deployed the slogan: 'The taste you hate twice a day.'

However, despite the many successful examples of frank candour, there are times when honesty is not the best policy. Of course, if there is a serious and indisputable flaw with a product then it needs to be recognized and addressed by brand managers, so that they can move on to a more positive message. But if it is only an honest but negative *opinion* that is being expressed, it usually causes brand damage.

As Ries and Trout themselves acknowledge, 'the law of candour must be used carefully and with great skill.' To understand what can happen when great skill is not deployed, you could do worse than ask Gerald Ratner.

During the 1980s he built his Ratner's business into the world's biggest brand of jewellery, through a series of publicity stunts and takeover deals. In 1991, however, Ratner managed to destroy his brand in the space of a sentence. In a speech to the Institute of Directors in London, he said the secret to Ratner's success was that many of its items of jewellery were 'total crap'. He also joked that Ratners earrings were likely to last for less time than a Marks & Spencer sandwich. Although the room filled with laughter, Ratner's investors and customers couldn't see the joke. Shortly afterwards he backtracked, saying that he was referring only to a very few items, but the damage had been done.

The Ratner's brand name was now synonymous with 'crap' products and a lack of respect for its customers. The company's share price plummeted from £2 to less than 8p, and consumer confidence sank without trace. Group profits fell from £112 million in 1991 to losses of £122 million a year later. 'Consumers would have been totally embarrassed and humiliated to have bought its product. It just became impossible,' says Tom Blackett, group deputy chairman of London-based branding consultancy Interbrand.

Gerald Ratner, and his eponymous brand of jewellery, were forced to make an exit. Shortly after he left the jewellery trade, he took part in an interview and appeared to be taking the situation in his stride. 'Someone said he had met comedians who wanted to be millionaires, but I must have been the only millionaire who wanted to be a comedian,' he told the interviewer. However, in 2002 Ratner was back on a mission to resurrect the Ratner's name and create an online version of the brand, called simply Ratners-Online.

'I didn't want to use the Ratner's name but research shows that it is still the best-known name in the jewellery business despite the fact that there hasn't been a Ratner's shop for years,' Gerald told the *Evening Standard* in 2001. In another interview, for the *Guardian*, he said the name would provoke curiosity from Web users. 'We were going to call it something else but thought it was more likely to get hits on the Internet – even from a curiosity point of view.'

Whether this curiosity will be converted into long-term sales remains to be seen. Gerald also needs to make sure that this time he keeps his foot a good distance away from his mouth. 'It is difficult for me to resist jokes, even if I am the only one that really finds them funny,' he chuckles. 'But I really will try.'

Lessons from Ratners

- *Think before you speak.* It often takes years to build trust among consumers, but as Gerald Ratner proved, that trust can be blown in a couple of words.
- *Remember that most dangers come from within.* Most brand damage does not arise from product flaws or distribution problems. A lot of it comes from employees or managers who fail to live up to their role as ambassadors of the brand. In service industries, where most employees are interacting with the public on a regular basis, it is especially important to maintain a positive attitude.

69 Planet Hollywood

Big egos, weak brand

Celebrity endorsements can help greatly in boosting sales of a product or service. For instance, when Oprah Winfrey recommended books via her branded book club, they were guaranteed bestseller status. Some brands also benefit from having their founder evolve into a celebrity, à la Richard Branson.

Then there are cases of celebrities turning their hand to business ventures. David Bowie lent his name to USABancshares.com, an Internet bank where you could get Bowie-branded cheque books and credit cards. Manchester United's Sir Alex Ferguson was a shareholder at toptable.co.uk, a restaurant information and booking service. U2 own a hotel and a nightclub. Bill Wyman owned his own restaurant.

One of the most famous of these celebrity-backed ventures was the Hollywood-themed eaterie, Planet Hollywood. Boasting such high-profile investors as Bruce Willis, Demi Moore, Whoopi Goldberg, Arnold Schwarzenegger and Sylvester Stallone, the chain was guaranteed maximum exposure when it launched in 1991. The company expanded quickly and soon had nearly 80 restaurants worldwide. In 1999, however, the company went bankrupt and numerous restaurants were shut down.

'Planet Hollywood has gone belly up,' declared wine critic Malcolm Gluck in the *Guardian*. 'Cows, vegetarians, food critics and assorted jealous restaurateurs will be rejoicing at the news that the most hyped chain of eateries in the history of cuisine has been roasted alive.' As soon as the news was out, Planet Hollywood lost even more customers and kept going in only a few of its original locations, with help of new investors from Saudi Arabia who made a relatively modest investment in the company.

So how could a brand that had achieved such exposure flop within less than a decade?

Firstly, the company expanded too quickly, launching new restaurants before seeing a profit in its original venues. The original plan was to open 300 branches by 2003.

Another factor was the food. Most people who eat out go because of the food, but Planet Hollywood never advertised this aspect of its business. In order to achieve long-term success, food or drink has to be the theme. Even McDonald's is about the food, even if it's the cost and convenience of it rather than the taste.

At best, Planet Hollywood attracted once-only visitors, lured by the novelty factor. 'The magnet is purely that of being seen at such a place and seeing what other hip characters are there,' wrote Malcolm Gluck. 'The hope that one might catch a glimpse of the backers or the backers' friends or celebrity hangers-on (who flock to the opening because of the chance of publicity and free food and drink but are never seen again).' But this is not the basis upon which to build a long-term business with repeat custom, which any restaurant must have in order to survive, let alone expand. 'It is great for tourists,' said Richard Harden, co-editor of Harden's London restaurant guides. 'Or for those who want a day out with the kids. But it is a one-off. A case of "been there, done that". There is no reason why the public should come back.'

Lessons from Planet Hollywood

- *Celebrity isn't enough.* 'These bozos thought, cynically, it was enough to trade on their Hollywood backgrounds. Bad move, fellas,' wrote Malcolm Gluck.
- *Word-of-mouth is crucial.* Word-of-mouth is more important than advertising and media exposure when it comes to eating out.
- *The theme should be tied to the core product.* Food, rather than an abstract notion of 'Hollywood', should have been the theme.

70 Fashion Café

From catwalk to catfights

Although it eventually proved to be a flop, Planet Hollywood spawned a number of imitators. David Hasselhoff tried to launch a Baywatch Café chain complete with waitresses in red swimsuits. Magician David Copperfield reportedly ploughed millions into a magic-themed restaurant chain which later vanished in a puff of smoke. Steven Spielberg invested in Dive, a submarine-shaped restaurant in Los Angeles with a giant cinema screen, taking diners on undersea voyages. It sank without trace.

One of the most spectacular of these Planet Hollywood-inspired failures was the Fashion Café, launched in 1995 by supermodels Naomi Campbell, Christy Turlington, Claudia Schiffer and Elle MacPherson. However, the chain, with its main branches in London and New York, struggled from the start. The connection between models and food was not an obvious one, and 'fashion' was not a theme that made people feel hungry.

As soon as the disappointing figures were in, the drama really started. Elle MacPherson and Naomi Campbell publicly accused founder Tomasso Buti of encouraging them to invest in the chain only to see US $25 million 'vanish' from the account books. Then Claudia Schiffer walked out of the venture, blaming 'old problems' with Naomi. 'Instead of promoting our cafés Naomi only thinks about collecting lovers,' Claudia told Italian newspaper *Il Messaggero*. 'We agreed to make more presentations for our group, but Naomi is always on a yacht with some boyfriend.' Naomi wasn't slow to respond in an interview with *The Sun*. 'Greed is a bad adviser,' she remarked. 'Claudia is wrong to leave the business. And it's not true that I have abandoned the promotional side.'

The infighting may have helped to sell newspapers but it did nothing for the brand. Although some branches turned an operating profit most failed to cover all their start-up costs. In 1998, three years after opening, it was time to call in the receivers.

Lessons from Fashion Café

- *Don't follow a failing formula.* Planet Hollywood was already struggling in 1995 when the Fashion Café was launched.
- *Have a logical brand association.* Models and food didn't really gel together.
- *Don't bitch about your colleagues.* It will only make the wrong sort of press headlines.

71 Hear'Say

From pop to flop

The UK reality TV show, *Popstars*, was the first programme to document the making of a band from obscurity to pop superstardom. The aim was to create a pop 'brand' that would not only be able to sell albums and singles, but also a wide variety of merchandise.

Hear'Say was the end product – consisting of brand members Noel Sullivan, Danny Foster, Suzanne Shaw, Myleene Klass and Kym Marsh. Their first hit, 'Pure and Simple', released in March 2001, became the fastest selling single in UK music history, with sales of over 1.2 million copies. The first album, 'Popstars', also went to number one and a 36-date tour was sold out.

However, as the memory of the TV show started to fade, so did public interest. The strength of the Hear'Say brand suddenly seemed to be in doubt. The band's second album was a complete flop and they started to get heckled at public appearances.

As the band had been completely manufactured (none of the members had known each other before the TV show), relationships within Hear'Say soon broke down. As a result of constant bickering, Kym Marsh left the band at the beginning of 2002.

After she had left, the band made the mistake of holding a supposedly 'public' audition for her replacement only to employ one of their dancers, Johnny Shentall. This generated even more bad headlines.

Then, on 1 October 2002 a statement from their record company Polydor confirmed that the band was splitting. The statement explained 'they felt they had lost the support of the public and Hear'Say had come to a natural end.' The band members also told the media that they were tired of getting abuse from the public, which made their lives 'hell'. Suzanne Shaw told *The Sun* newspaper that their pop brand fell victim to the fickle nature of fashion. 'It's like a pair of trainers: one minute they're in and the next minute they're out,' she said.

So while the *Popstars* phenomenon continued to be a success, spawning shows such as *Pop Idol* and *Popstars: The Rivals* in the UK and *American Idol* in the US, the pop brand it created was on a downward slope almost from its conception.

Lessons from Hear'Say

- *Hype can turn against you.* At the start of 2001 Hear'Say was the most hyped band never to have released a single. However, the weight of the media interest soon turned against them to crush the brand.
- *Have something to unify your brand.* The Spice Girls weathered Geri Halliwell's departure (at least in the short term) by rallying behind the 'Girl Power' banner, but as the *Guardian* reported 'poor Hear'Say, only in it for the fame, didn't have so much as a slogan to stand on.'

72 Guiltless Gourmet

Helping the competition

Although most people failures are a result of unscrupulous decisions or vicious personality clashes, on rare occasions people let their brands down despite having the best of intentions. This is what happened to Michael P Schall's brand, Guiltless Gourmet, when he gave away the secrets of his success to his chief competition.

In the 1990s, Guiltless Gourmet was a small business success story which attracted a great deal of attention in its native Texas. The company, which made baked, low-fat tortilla chips, had evolved in the space of five years from being a home-based operation into a US $23 million business with a massive factory.

In addition to media support, the company also had endorsement from such lofty US health authorities as the Center for Science in the Public Interest, which supported claims that the Guiltless Gourmet range was a healthy – indeed 'guiltless' – alternative to other snack brands.

As is so often the case, Guiltless Gourmet soon became a victim of its own success. Frito-Lay, one of the largest US companies producing snack-food (and normally of the 'guilt-filled' rather than 'guiltless' variety) had watched the phenomenal growth of this small Texan company and wanted a piece of the action.

Schall, the owner of Guiltless Gourmet, had worked as a consultant for Frito-Lay, and had even invited the company to acquire the brand. But Frito-Lay hadn't warmed to that idea. Instead, it wanted to create an entirely new tortilla brand to take on Guiltless Gourmet. And given Frito-Lay's well-established distribution network, it wasn't too long before its new product – low-fat Baked Tostitos – was available in supermarkets across the United States. Straightaway, Frito-Lay's offering was chomping its way through Guiltless Gourmet's market share. Within a year, Guiltless Gourmet's revenues reduced to US $9 million, and the company was forced to shut down its factory and start outsourcing. Its workforce slimmed down from 125 to 10 employees.

Although it is easy to see this situation as unavoidable from Guiltless Gourmet's perspective, there are always ways in which a brand can protect itself from outside threats. For instance, some have said that Guiltless should have broadened its product line into other relevant categories or outsourced production at an earlier stage.

There is also the issue of Schall's decision to work with Frito-Lay as a consultant. When *Business Week* magazine enquired, Frito-Lay wouldn't discuss the aborted buy-out nor the suggestion that it may have just been scouting for competitive intelligence. Of course, we can only assume that Frito-Lay are 'guiltless' but even they admit that the information provided by Guiltless Gourmet was helpful. 'Guiltless Gourmet provided us with a great benchmark to get our product better-tasting,' admitted Frito-Lay spokeswoman Lynn Markley.

Although Guiltless Gourmet's low fat tortilla chips are still on sale, the future of the brand is still in doubt. Schall still believes the best route may rest with a buyout. 'Our brand has great value,' he told *Business Week*. 'It would be good to become part of an organisation where that brand can be leveraged.'

Lessons from Guiltless Gourmet

- *Be aware that success breeds competition.* Guiltless Gourmet's success within a niche product category was inevitably going to catch the attention of larger rivals.
- *Have a Plan B.* Brands need to prepare for such an eventuality and have a back-up plan.

CHAPTER 8

Rebranding failures

Brands, like people, have a fear of the ageing process. They don't want to grow old, because growing old means growing stale and once a brand has become old and stale it is as good as dead.

So how do brands delay the ageing process? Like people in the same situation, brands facing their mid-life crisis resort to drastic measures in order to stay young and relevant. Typical methods include changing their name, changing their overall look and even changing their brand 'philosophy'. In order not to become old and tired, many companies embark on rebranding exercises to make themselves look more up-to-date and relevant to their target market.

Another reason to rebrand products is to make them fit with a global identity. For instance, in the UK Mars rebranded Opal Fruits and Marathon so that they had the same names as in the rest of the world. Hence they were changed to Starburst and Snickers, respectively. Although both brand make-overs were unpopular at the time, neither product lost out in terms of sales.

However, sometimes the decisions have to be reversed. When the chocolate covered rice cereal Coco Pops had its name changed to Choco Krispies, a national poll discovered 92 per cent of Britons were unhappy about the change. Coco Pops returned and did better than ever.

Yet while the risks are great, rebranding remains more popular than ever. In the United States there are now around 3,000 company name changes every year. In 1990, the figure was closer to 1,000. The need to stay ahead means companies are prepared to gamble away their history and heritage for the promise of future profits.

'Whatever made you successful in the past, won't in the future,' were the wise words of Leo Platt, CEO of Hewlett Packard. If you stand still you will fall behind, seems to be the general message. Indeed, many of the most successful brands today retain their prominent position by evolving and updating their identity over time.

But while there is no denying that market trends now move faster than ever, companies that don't think carefully before rebranding can risk undermining their previous marketing efforts. 'Be sure to use research to consult your customers, as marketers are often so close to the brand that at times they can see a problem where there isn't one,' says Richard Duncan, managing director of South African marketing consultancy TBWA. 'Whatever you do, be careful not to undermine the fundamental values and strengths of your brand and ensure that whatever you do is in sync with your business rationale and aims.'

While this sounds painfully obvious, there are enough examples of rebranding disasters to prove that it isn't as easy as it sounds. After all, brands create an emotional connection with the consumer. Ever since the legendary adman Bruce Barton famously transformed General Motors into 'something personal, warm and human' in the 1920s, branding has been about creating an emotional bond. The company may believe it owns the brand, but it doesn't own the feelings that the brand manages to generate.

Okay, so people won't fall apart if their favourite breakfast cereal changes its name, but they won't like it, unless they asked for it to be changed. So a company is left with two options. Either it can make changes so subtle that the consumer will hardly notice (for example, the Shell logo has had over 20 subtle design updates, none of which have radically changed the company's identity), or it must make sure that the changes it makes are in accordance with the customer's wishes.

If a company ignores both options and makes changes for the simple reason that this makes sense for the company, then it may end up following in the same ill-fated footsteps of the brands featured in this chapter.

73 Consignia

A post office by any other name

When the UK state-owned Post Office Group decided to change its brand identity, a new name was the first on the shopping list. The reason for the brand makeover was partly to do with the fact that the 300-year-old Post Office Group was no longer simply a mail-only organization. It had logistics and customer call centre operations, and was planning a number of acquisitions abroad. There was also growing public confusion about what the purpose of the organization's three arms – post offices, Parcel Force, Royal Mail – actually was.

'We were researching hard into what this organization called the Post Office was facing,' explained Keith Wells to BBC Online. Wells was from Dragon Brands, the brand consultancy that helped to repackage the organization. 'What we needed was something that could help pull all the bits together.'

The consultancy considered the name of each division but none was appropriate. The name 'Post Office' was dismissed as 'too generic'. 'Parcel Force' was, again, inappropriate. So what about 'Royal Mail?' 'That has problems when operating in countries which have their own royal family, or have chopped the heads off their royals,' said Wells. So Dragon Brands set about creating a new umbrella term for the whole organization. It wanted to come up with something non-specific, something which would work equally well throughout Europe, not just in the UK, and most of all something which didn't tie the Post Office Group down to mail.

There is a wise logic behind such thinking. After all, many companies have come unstuck as time moves on and their name is no longer relevant. For instance, Carphone Warehouse may have once imagined a world full of consumers waiting to upgrade their carphones, but the reality is that now most people wouldn't recognize a carphone if it hit them over the head. And other brands have managed to create very successful identities with brand names that have no direct relevance to their products, or anyone else's products for that matter. This is especially true on the Internet. While self-descriptive brands such as Letsbuyit.com and Pets.com flopped, vague and mysterious brand names such as Amazon, Google and Yahoo! have worked exceptionally well. Indeed, many of the largest brands in the world follow this model. To take the most obvious example, no-one who spends their money via Richard Branson's company expects to take home a real virgin, any more than people buying books at Amazon expect to be transported to a tropical rainforest. These names are about evocation. They are about the identity of the brand, not the product.

Before the Post Office, many other British institutions had also tried to bring themselves into the new millennium. British Steel had become 'Corus' following its merger with Koninklijke Hoogovens. 'Centrica' was a former arm of British Gas. 'Thus' was the new name given to the telecoms division of Scottish Power. The list goes on and on.

So what was the name given to the Post Office? On 9 January 2002, the group's chief executive, John Roberts, stood outside his organization's headquarters and declared that the name was Consignia. This name, he added, was 'modern, meaningful and entirely appropriate' to the rapidly evolving organization.

Dragon Brand's Keith Wells was equally happy with Consignia. 'It's got consign in it. It's got a link with insignia, so there is this kind of royalty-ish thing in the back of one's mind,' he explained to the BBC. 'And there's this lovely dictionary definition of consign which is "to entrust to the care of." That goes right back to sustaining trust, which was very, very important.' In addition, the name change had been approved by the controversial government minister Stephen Byers, who was at that time the trade secretary.

The reaction from the media and the general public was considerably less sympathetic. Some thought it sounded like a new brand of aftershave or deodorant. Others thought it was the name of an electricity company. The BBC's Web site referred to 'the most notorious ever Post Office robbery – that of the name itself.' The Web site also asked the British public to e-mail their opinions of the name. Their responses were almost unanimously critical of the re-brand.

'Consignia doesn't sound like the national institution that the Royal Mail does. Instead, it reminds me of that brand of anti-perspirant, called Insignia,' wrote one.

'It's a poor excuse to say that Royal Mail could be confusing when it takes a paragraph to explain what Consignia means,' wrote another.

One respondent e-mailed in with his tongue firmly in cheek saying that 'given the current crisis within the Post Office, Consignia Plc seems like an excellent name. It is an anagram of Panic Closing.'

Soon it became clear that the name change was not having a positive effect. Although the Post Office had shifted to become a plc, the public still felt it belonged to them. If they didn't like the new name, they therefore felt it was their right to be angry.

As the Post Office's corporate performance started to falter, the name was blamed even more. 'The name got muddied with the comments that business is doing appallingly – this idea that nothing had been the same since the name change. It's a soft target,' said Wells.

Soft target or not, May 2002 saw a U-turn as the new Consignia chairman Allan Leighton confirmed the name was to go – 'probably in less than two years.' He also admitted that he hated the name. 'There's not really a commercial reason to do it, but there's a credibility reason to do it,' he told BBC TV's Breakfast with Frost programme. He said the name change was 'unfortunate' as it had coincided with a period of underperformance by the company (it lost over one million pounds a day during one month in 2001).

However, the news was lost on some people, as the Consignia brand had failed to become a household name. 'I didn't know that the Post Office wasn't called the Post Office,' one member of the public told a radio news interviewer at the time of the announcement. 'Everyone I know calls it the Post Office.'

Lessons from Consignia

- *Don't change for the sake of change.* The public perception was that the whole rebranding exercise was pointless. This impression was confirmed by a lack of advertising. 'We thought what would be the point of advertising if all you would be saying is this name change is happening which is not going to affect you?' justifies Dragon Brands' Keith Wells.
- *Realize that business realities have an impact.* The new brand suffered due to the fact it coincided with a poor period of corporate performance.

74 Tommy Hilfiger

The power of the logo

Tommy Hilfiger is one of the world's best-loved designer clothing brands. During the 1990s Tommy Hilfiger moved from being a small, niche brand targeting upper class US consumers to becoming a global powerhouse with broad youth appeal.

But then, in 2000, the brand was suddenly in trouble. From a high of US $40 per share in May 1999, Tommy Hilfiger's share price fell to US $22.62 on New Year's Day 2000, and was cut in half again by the end of that year. Sales were slowing and, most tellingly, flagship stores in London and Beverly Hills closed down. Various runway shows at fashion events worldwide were also cancelled.

So what was going wrong? According to Tommy Hilfiger himself, the explanation is to be found in his decision to be adventurous with the brand. He said in a 2001 interview with *New York* magazine:

> At one point, I told my people, 'We have to be the first with trends', so we ran out and tried to do the coolest, most advanced clothes. We didn't just do denim embroidery. We jewelled it. We studded it. We really pushed the envelope because we thought our customer would respond. But the customer did not respond in a big way, and our business last year – men's, women's, junior's – suffered as a result.

Part of this 'pushing the envelope' strategy involved reworking the brand's famous imagery. Tommy Hilfiger, more than any other brand in the fashion industry, is a brand based on a logo. Indeed, some of the company's most successful products have been T-shirts with the red-white-and-blue logo emblazoned across them. Everything about the logo, from the primary colours to the capital letters shouting TOMMY HILFIGER, suggested a bold, brash and 100 per cent US identity. When you wore a Tommy Hilfiger T-shirt everybody knew exactly what you were wearing, so long as they could read.

Of course, these logo-centric US brand values had been present in other fashion labels – most obviously Calvin Klein and Ralph Lauren – but Tommy Hilfiger had taken it a step further. And by 1999, Hilfiger himself was starting to feel it may have been a step too far. 'When business plateaued in 1999,' he explained, 'we thought the customer didn't want the Tommy logo any-more. So we took it off a lot of stuff. We made it tiny. We became very insecure about being a red-white-and-blue logo brand. We thought we had to be much chic-er, more in line with the Euro houses like Gucci and Prada.'

In other words, Tommy Hilfiger abandoned the values that had built the brand. Of course, the brand had in many senses become credible in high fashion circles but this credibility arrived, in part at least, by the brand's urban appeal. In *No Logo* (written before Tommy Hilfiger's dip in fortunes), Naomi Klein explored the twin identity of the Tommy brand: 'Tommy Hilfiger, even more than Nike or Adidas, has turned the harnessing of ghetto cool into a mass-marketing science. Hilfiger forged a formula that has since been imitated by Polo, Nautica, Munsingwear and several other clothing com-panies looking for a short cut to making it at the suburban mall with inner-city attitude.'

However, this twin identity (suburbia meets the inner-city) happened initially by accident. In the beginning, Tommy Hilfiger produced clothes for the 'preppy' market, falling somewhere between the Gap and Ralph Lauren. Pretty soon though, the hip-hop community embraced the label, and the Hilfiger logo could be seen popping up on every other rap video. It was only later that Hilfiger deliberately designed clothes for this market. In effect, this meant accentuating what was already there – making the prominent logo even more prominent, and the baggy T-shirts even baggier.

This strategy proved successful because the company was only exaggerating a formula that was already there. In 1999 though, the formula was aband-oned completely, and, because of this, it strayed from the original preppy-style that had made the brand so strong originally. For instance, Hilfiger launched a 'Red Label' sub-brand aimed at the very top of the market. This logoless range included such garments as US $7,000 patchwork, python-skin trousers. Clearly these items were out of the reach of the average Tommy Hilfiger customer. Another bad move was the decision to place stores in locations such as London's Bond Street and Beverly Hills' Rodeo Drive. 'The London flagship store wasn't open for a year when we realised we had made a mistake,' he said in the *New York* magazine interview. 'And the average age on Rodeo Drive is probably 50 years old. My customers are much younger than that. We thought all the cool people in LA come to Rodeo. But they don't.'

Since 2001 though, Tommy Hilfiger has been learning from his mistakes and going back to basics. 'As a result of learning from our errors, we went back to our roots: classics with a twist. We're about colour, we're about preppy, we're about classic, we're about America!' And as a result of this turnaround, customers and investors alike are again comfortable with the Tommy Hilfiger brand. 'It will never again be the hot, sexy, overly talked-about, flashy, zippy, fast-growing company it was, but it will be a damn nice company with lots of cash,' observed one Wall Street analyst at the time of the turnaround. 'What you've got now is a company that went from an A-plus to an F-minus. And now it's going back to a B. And it's a hell of a business as a B.'

Lessons from Tommy Hilfiger

- *Don't deviate from your formula.* Known as the brand which produces 'classic with a twist', Hilfiger concentrated too much on the 'twist' and not enough on the 'classic'.
- *Don't compete with irrelevant rivals.* Tommy Hilfiger attempting to compete with successful European high fashion brands such as Gucci and Prada on their own terms was a mistake which even Hilfiger himself has acknowledged.
- *Don't over-extend the brand.* During its bad patch, Tommy Hilfiger moved into a lot of new product categories for which it wasn't suited.
- *Don't be scared of your logo.* The logo is what made Tommy Hilfiger the brand it is today. In fact, the Tommy Hilfiger brand is pure logo. When the logo disappeared or was toned down, the brand ran into trouble.

75 BT Cellnet to O_2

Undoing the brand

In September 2001, UK mobile phone operator BT Cellnet announced it was getting rid of its brand name in favour of a new international identity. The decision followed a continuing drop in its market share of call revenues. Furthermore, BT Cellnet's arch-rival Orange (often admired for its brand name) increased its revenues and knocked BT Cellnet into third place, behind both Orange and Vodafone. Cellnet's first parent company, British Telecom, had sold off its mobile operation and the new owners felt no reason to stick with the struggling identity.

When the announcement to scrap the brand name was made, analysts agreed it might be the right move. 'Cellnet had a head start being part of BT but it has somewhat sat on its laurels,' said Louisa Greenacre, telecoms analyst at ING Barings. 'Orange has been more aggressive, while Cellnet has not got its branding strategy right, particularly as the brand Genie, BT's mobile phone Internet portal, is slightly distracting.' She added that BT Cellnet's strategy, similar to many mobile operators, had been to grow a customer base as quickly as possible, but brand loyalty would be the key to increasing average revenues from that user base.

The new brand name was O_2, the chemical symbol for Oxygen. 'We have chosen a name that is modern and universal,' said Peter Erskine, chief executive of the mobile business. The new name spelt the end for the variety of brands carried by the BT Wireless Group. These included Cellnet in the UK, VIAG Interkom in Germany, Telfort in the Netherlands and Digifone in the Republic of Ireland. The Genie mobile Internet portal was also to be relabelled.

So why O_2? 'Oxygen is the key thing to life and you don't have to teach people to spell it,' explained Peter Erskine. 'There were hundreds of names to start with and O_2 leapt off the pages fairly early. It's a universal term. We wanted something that was easy, clean and fresh.'

The branding exercise was viewed as all-important, both inside and outside the company. 'Brands are now being measured in a way they haven't been measured before,' one analyst told the *Telegraph*. 'They're not seen as a nice accessory, they're seen as a valued part of the business.'

BT Cellnet was a confusing brand, complicated by BT's other UK mobile brand identity, Genie. When British Telecom sold off its mobile operation, the new owners felt the name-change would help to forge a clearer, more relevant identity. But did it?

The early signs are that it didn't. Indeed, despite a massive marketing campaign including sponsorship of the TV show *Big Brother*, many are unfamiliar with the name. According to a poll conducted by Continental Research for their Summer 2002 Mobile Report, almost eight in ten BT Cellnet subscribers did not realize the service had been renamed O_2. 'The decision of the new owner to abandon the brand has left customers – many of whom are older executives who were the first to buy mobiles – unimpressed,' reported the *Guardian*. 'This does suggest there has been some difficulty communicating the change of name to current users of the O_2 network,' agreed Colin Shaddick, the director of Continental Research.

Lessons from BT Cellnet

- *Don't overlap brand identities.* When BT set up different mobile businesses with different names, such as Cellnet and Genie, it created consumer confusion.
- *Realize that brand names can't be 'undone' overnight.* Despite investing millions into the name change, O_2 remains unfamiliar to many mobile users.

76 ONdigital to ITV Digital

How the 'beautiful dream' went sour

In 1998, a new UK digital TV channel was introduced which aimed to take on Rupert Murdoch's BSkyB and convert millions of middle-England viewers to pay-television with a new platform accessible via set-top boxes – digital terrestrial television. In 2002, however, it went out of business.

'We thought we could take on Sky, through its Achilles heel: it was the least trusted by the audience,' says Marc Sands, the first director of brand marketing for ONdigital. 'We would differentiate ourselves by our behaviour, clarity, and transparency of prices. That was the beautiful dream. Plug and play.'

However, it soon became clear that it would be difficult to deliver the special software and set-top boxes, and cope with patchy coverage across the country. 'By summer 1999, I saw that the problems were terminal,' says Sands. 'For those for whom it didn't work, when the pictures froze, the promise was shattered. We never got past first base.'

Then the company's chief rival, BSkyB, raised the pressure by paying retailers money to recommend its system. BSkyB's decision to give away free set-top boxes meant ONdigital had little choice but to follow suit, a move that cost an extra £100 million a year. 'I think the decision by ONdigital to go head-to-head with BSkyB was probably a mistake,' said Chris Smith, former secretary of state for Culture, Media and Sport (who oversaw the government's digital plans until June 2001), in an interview with the *Guardian*. 'They should have aimed for a different part of the market.'

In 2001, ONdigital was rebranded ITV Digital, linking it to an established and trusted brand name (ITV remains the most popular terrestrial channel in the UK). However, the same problem remained. Viewers needed to buy completely new equipment, which didn't require a dish. In other words, it was a completely new platform.

The technical problems were also an issue. The software used in the set-top boxes didn't have enough memory and crashed frequently. As former customer Bridget Furst explains:

> I signed up for ONdigital in November 1999 as we live in a conserva-tion area and were told we couldn't have a dish. But all the technical breakdowns drove us dotty. The picture would freeze without warning, three or four times a week. You had to phone for advice, give your security password, queue for technical assistance, and then you needed 15 fingers to put things right. I was told that their software couldn't cope with the BBC channels on the platform.

Graham Simcocks, the company's director until 2001, realizes that the technological issues hindered development. 'The business failed to take seriously enough the whole range of technological issues: why the picture kept disappearing, the need to boost its power. That was the biggest reason for customers being put off. Then there were homes that were supposed to be within a reception area but still had problems,' he says.

Another factor was the lack of incentive to buy ITV Digital. Although ITV's major networks Carlton and Granada were behind the company, they didn't provide exclusive access to their major programmes. 'I think Carlton and Granada didn't support it enough,' says former ITV Digital sales director Matthew Seaman. 'They should have given it more exclusive programmes. First runs of *Coronation Street*. Why not? Pay-television isn't something that just happens. It needed a huge, bold move, equivalent to Sky's Premier League. But the shareholders never felt they could risk the ITV crown jewels.'

Few could understand exactly the point of the network. At first, it had clearly tried to differentiate itself from BSkyB. Stephen Grabiner, ITV Digital's first chief executive, once referred to Murdoch's multi-channel vision for digital television as of interest only to 'sad people who live in lofts.' However, ITV Digital later mimicked BSkyB's football-centric strategy, by paying £315 million for the rights to televise matches from the Nationwide Football League. They also ended up buying movies from the satellite firm. 'The inherent contradictions from the top down confused viewers,' reckoned *The Observer* newspaper.

The Observer also pointed the finger at Charles Allen and Michael Green, the chairmen of the platform's two shareholders, Granada and Carlton, and the other management figures:

> Many in the City expect that, even if Allen and Green manage to hang on to their positions, allowing them to make a more leisurely exit later in the year, some of their lieutenants will soon have to fall on their swords. Question marks hang over the head of Granada chief executive Steve Morrison, who, at the height of negotiations with the Football League, opted to take a holiday in New Zealand. And it is hard to see how Stuart Prebble, a former journalist who, despite having no experience in the pay TV arena, rose to become chief executive of ITV and ITV Digital, can stay in the ITV fold.

But alongside managerial failings, some things were beyond the company's control. For instance, despite assurances from the Independent Television Commission (ITC) that the power of ITV Digital's broadcasting signal would be increased, nothing happened. Coverage was reduced to include only about half of the UK. Also, the ITC's decision to force Sky out of the original consortium – over 'fears of a Murdoch dominated media' according to *The Observer* – meant that none of the companies behind the platform had solid expertise within the pay-TV arena.

'The ITC kept Sky out. If Sky had been allowed to stay in, ITV Digital would have got to three million subscribers by now,' said Dermont Nolan of media consultancy TBS in April 2002. That some month ITV Digital met its demise and called in the administrators from Deloitte and Touche. Although there were over 100 expressions of interest in the platform's assets most of the interest was to do with the brand's mascot, the ITV Digital monkey which became something of a celebrity in a series of adverts featuring comedian Johnny Vegas. Unfortunately, the monkey's popularity didn't rub off on the platform it was promoting.

Lessons from ONdigital/ITV Digital

- *Be available*. Technological problems meant that the platform wasn't available in many parts of the UK.
- *Be reliable*. These same problems led to a reputation for unreliability.
- *Have a strong incentive*. ITV Digital didn't simply require people to switch channels. They needed to go out and get completely new technology to place on top of their TVs. To do that, they needed a very strong incentive – the ability to watch something they loved, which they couldn't find elsewhere.
- *Deliver on your promises*. 'ITV Digital's promises ran ahead of its ability to deliver, it was a totally new system,' says Marc Sands, the platform's first director of brand marketing.
- *Don't tarnish related brands*. 'The greatest mistake was to rebrand it ITV Digital, dragging ITV, one of the strongest consumer brands, into disrepute,' says Sands.
- *Be realistic*. 'I know what it costs to set up digital transmitters,' says Gerald H David, chairman of Aerial Facilities, experts in digital radio engineering. 'ITV Digital's demise is all part of a pretty unrealistic plan. The ITC put the cart before the horse when it licensed it.'
- *Understand the competition*. 'Carlton and Granada didn't anticipate such a competitive environment,' says John Egan, director of operations and strategy for the platform until 1999.

77 Windscale to Sellafield

Same identity, different name

At the risk of understating the case, nuclear energy has always had something of an image problem. When incidents happen at nuclear plants this 'problem' becomes a nightmare.

For instance, when massive amounts of radioactive material were released from the UK's Windscale atomic works in 1957, following a serious fire, the consequences were disastrous. The local community in Cumbria were understandably terrified about the health implications of uncontained radiation.

Rather than close the plant down, the government believed the best way to put distance between the disaster and the nuclear plant as a whole was to change the name, from Windscale to Sellafield. However, everybody knew that the nuclear facility was essentially the same, and so all the negative associations were simply transferred to the new name. The name-change certainly didn't stop the rise in health problems in the area as this 1999 article from a local Cumbria newspaper testifies:

> While animals are still being irradiated in laboratories all over the country to 'study' the effects, Dr Martin Gardner and colleagues of the Medical Research Council in Southampton have learned that the children of fathers who worked at the Sellafield nuclear-reprocessing plant were six times more likely to be afflicted by leukaemia than

neighbours whose fathers had not worked at the plant. Sellafield, formerly called Windscale, has experienced so many episodes of radioactive leakage that the government changed the name to disassociate the plant from its history. There is an unusually high incidence of childhood leukaemia in the area. Dr Gardner's study seems to indicate that it is caused by damaged sperm, which leaves the father intact but visits the government's sins upon unborn children.

The new epithet therefore failed to generate any increase in goodwill towards the plant. Julian Gorham, creative head of the Brand Naming Company, claims that name changes are pointless without meaningful organizational changes. 'Windscale, Sellafield, it's the same thing isn't it? Nothing has changed.'

Lessons from Windscale/Sellafield

- *Change needs to be fundamental.* A name change won't fool anybody if the procedures remain unchanged.
- *You can't hide your history.* Everybody in Cumbria knew about the 1957 incident, regardless of the new name, as its consequences were still felt for many years.

Over the following pages are even more of the most notable rebranding misses.

78 Payless Drug Store to Rite Aid

In 1998, Payless Drug Store, a regional chain of chemists operating across western USA, changed its name to Rite Aid Corporation. The name change required several million dollars spent on advertising just to gain a level of local awareness equivalent to the previous brand name. The reason for the change was the acquisition of the Payless Drug Store by the Rite Aid Corporation, which owned its own brand of chemists throughout the United States. They therefore thought the re-brand was a logical step. But what happened? Soon after the Rite Aid acquisition and brand conversion most of the former Payless stores started to lose 10 per cent of sales every month. Eventually Rite Aid sold 38 of the stores in California, cut down its workforce, and realigned its West Coast distribution centre.

79 British Airways

When British Airways went through an expensive rebranding exercise in 1996, it couldn't have picked a worse time. The media contrasted the costly makeover with the 'cost-saving' redundancies announced shortly afterwards.

There was also criticism about the nature of the new identity. The airline had abandoned the Union Jack colours on the tail-fin, and replaced them with a series of different images representing a more international identity. Many saw this move as unpatriotic, and Richard Branson, boss of the company's arch-rival Virgin Atlantic, was quick to rub salt in the wounds by painting Union Jacks on its aircraft and using British Airways' former 'Fly the Flag' slogan. It wasn't long before British Airways scrapped the new and expensive tail-fin designs. Ironically, US customers and partners had stated to complain that they wanted Britain's flagship airline to look more British.

80 MicroPro

Remember MicroPro? In the 1980s, and even at the beginning of the 1990s, MicroPro made leading word processing software product, WordStar. The program was even heralded as 'one of the greatest single software efforts in the history of computing' by the widely respected technology expert, John C Dvorak.

Because of the popularity of the WordStar product, MicroPro rebranded themselves WordStar International. This move proved to be a major mistake. 'The new brand identity proved immediately self-limiting,' explains advertising copywriter John Kuraoka, in a white paper on branding. 'As WordStar International, the company was poorly positioned to keep up with changes in the computer industry – such as the rise of integrated software bundles that were the predecessors to today's Microsoft Office. Note that Microsoft never became 'Windows International'.' The WordStar name had quickly become an albatross around the company's neck. Between 1988 and 1993 the company struggled to find new ways to continue selling variations of the WordStar product. The rise of competitors such as Word Perfect and, later, Microsoft Word, led to WordStar's corresponding and rapid decline.

CHAPTER 9

Internet and new technology failures

On the Internet, brand failure has become the norm. Those companies that somehow manage to make a profit are considered freaks, while those that struggle month by month to stay alive are applauded for their efforts.

Such has been the lasting impact of the dot.com fallout which occurred at the turn of the millennium, the quickest way a brand can devalue its name is to add '.com' to the end of it. Yet paradoxically, those brands that ignore the Internet are also placing their reputations in jeopardy.

Just as the Internet is now a part of life, so it must be a part of brand-building. The danger is to treat it as an entirely separate entity rather than simply as another communications medium or sales channel. Of course, the Internet does have unique characteristics, which need to be acknowledged. It facilitates two-way communication. It also enables consumers with a grudge to spread their anti-brand message in a way not possible with traditional one-way media. Most significantly, it levels out the playing field. Competitors large and small, wherever they happen to be located, are within equal reach.

Due to the democratic nature of the Internet, even the smallest of companies can eventually become the biggest brands. This is because having a unique approach is far more effective than spending millions on online and offline advertising. Furthermore, because of the immediacy of the Internet the value of a great concept can be spread around the world in a matter of minutes.

Whereas for the industrial age choice meant 'any colour so long as it's black', on the Internet users are presented with a kaleidoscopic range of possibilities. When Brand X fails to deliver, Brand Y is always only one click away. After all, if someone is visiting a site from a search engine (and most people do) they are likely to have a list of 10 or so other sites they want to visit. This means successful branding is more important than ever, in order to stand out from the competition.

As the Internet progresses there is a move away from thinking about 'eye-balls' to a concentration on relationships. Many leading e-business figures now believe brand development should be measured less in terms of how quickly a site can expand its customer base and more in terms of how existing customers decide to come back. As Rory Sutherland, executive director of Ogilvy One has put it: 'The Internet is about brand depth, not breadth. It's not worth chasing share of market, it's share of wallet that really counts. Once you have your loyal community, there are fabulous opportunities for cross-selling, personalised services and meeting the multiple needs of the same group.'

Not only does the Internet enable companies and their customers to engage in conversation with each other, but it also helps customers to talk to other customers about your company. As the Cluetrain Web site explains, 'Markets are conversations. Through the Internet, people are discovering and inventing new ways to share relevant knowledge with blinding speed. As a direct result, markets are getting smarter – and getting smarter faster than most companies.'

Prolific e-brands such as Amazon, eBay, Yahoo! and MSN have learnt that if visitors communicate with each other, it not only increases their loyalty to a site (and hence their 'lifetime value') but it also enables the brand to develop in line with the needs of the consumer by providing visitors with a platform on which they can voice their opinions on the brand. In some cases opinions aired in community forums have led to a radical rethinking of e-companies' marketing strategies.

For instance, when Amazon was toying with the idea of variable pricing, it decided to trial run the policy for one week on its DVD products only. Amazon then monitored its DVD Talk chat forum to try and gauge consumer response. When it spotted a handful of negative comments Amazon immediately announced that it was withdrawing the policy because, in the words of Amazon's chief executive Jeff Bezos, 'it created uncertainty for customers rather than simplifying their lives.' Amazon was therefore able to act quickly, before it became too heavily associated with what was appearing to be an unpopular move.

However, none of this means that the fundamental purpose of branding has changed. Daniel Letts, senior consultant at brand strategists Wolff Olins (who have clients like BT and Unilever), believes it is wrong to assume that branding online is incompatible with offline branding. 'The fact that people treated it so differently in the early days, is one of the reasons why so many online brands fared so badly. After all, we don't talk about 'TV brands' and treat Sky very differently because its primary channel is TV do we?'

As many customers' first experience of a brand is via the Net, it is best to view online branding as a confirmation of your overall brand identity, rather than as a quirky offshoot. It is also important to understand the potential brand damage that can be caused by the Internet.

On the Internet, there is less control over the brand message. If a business fails to inform the online public about a product flaw or a weakness in its service, consumers will be quick to inform each other. They can join a chat room, post a message to a discussion board or even set up their own Web site. Everyone is connected to everyone else and can make their opinion heard. This means that the perception of the brand has never been closer to the reality of the product or service as it is today. There is no fooling the target market.

The reason so many online brands have failed is that they have been blinded by the technology itself, and almost forgot the target market completely. When the crash began on New York's high tech Nasdaq market in March 2000, many online brands on both sides of the Atlantic were too weak to survive it. For many, simply to be a part of this online 'revolution' was enough. Success, it seemed, was guaranteed. This wasn't just a new channel for business, it was going to completely change the world.

However, as the Internet-related cases in this chapter illustrate, hard business realities were never as far away as the dot.com entrepreneurs had liked to think. Building technology brands isn't any more difficult than any other form of brand building, providing the relevant companies remember the lessons of those that have perished. If these lessons can be taken on board, failure may become the exception rather than the rule for technology brands.

81 Pets.com

In the mid-1990s, when the commercial potential for the Internet was beginning to be realized, people started to register Internet addresses with no intention of using them. This so-called land-grab was fuelled by a desire to sell these addresses at a later date.

Indeed, names such as business.com and sex.com proved to be so attractive to certain companies that millions were paid for the right to set up a Web site at that address. The belief was that if someone was looking for business information or pornography they would type a generic name into the address box in the assumption that it would lead to a relevant site, if not the *most* relevant site. It was also anticipated that such a name would be easy for Internet users to remember.

One of those who set about registering addresses was Pasadena-based entrepreneur, Greg McLemore. Among the hundreds of generic names he chose was Pets.com. However, instead of selling the name he decided to use it himself in a bid to target the highly lucrative US pet market.

This wasn't just going to be any old Internet company. Pets.com was set to be huge. Immediately after founding his venture McLemore relocated to San Francisco and went on the hunt for investment. In early 1999, he found it. Hummer Winblad Venture Partners, a highly respected venture capital firm based in Silicon Valley, liked what it saw and decided to fund the company.

So did Jeff Bezos, owner of a golden Labrador retriever and a certain online bookstore called Amazon.com, who was sold a 50 per cent stake in Pets.com. In a March 1999 statement to the press Bezos declared his enthusiasm. 'We invest only in companies that share our passion for customers,' he said.

'Pets.com has a leading market position, and its proven management team is dedicated to a great customer experience, whether it's making a product like a ferret hammock easy to find, or help in locating a pet-friendly hotel.'

Julie Wainwright, Pets.com's CEO and negotiator of the deal, was equally happy. 'This is a marriage made in heaven and clearly positions us as the online category leader. The successful investment track record represented by Amazon.com and Hummer Winblad really makes this a CEO's dream team.'

The press statement also included a statistic from the Pet Industry Joint Advisory Council which stated that in 1998, the US pet category was valued at US $23 billion. As the online leader of this sector, Pets.com was clearly set for success. After all, the Web users had already proved themselves willing to pay for books, CDs and software via the net, so why not pet products?

However, it soon became clear that Pets.com was not going to be the only major online player within the industry. Petopia.com, another San Francisco-based company, had managed to secure US $9 million from another high-profile venture capital firm, Technology Crossovers, who believed strongly in the pet market's online potential. It also gained investment from one of the leading 'real world' pet companies, Petco. Petco's longstanding rival PetsMart was equally keen to gain a piece of the action, and launched PetsMart.com. In addition, there was Petstore.com, backed by the Animal Planet cable network.

However, throughout 1999 Pets.com managed to keep a nose ahead of its three main competitors, securing a further US $50 million from investors. To gain further advantage it decided to cut its prices almost in half. Competing on price would never be enough though. If Pets.com was to stay in front of its rivals into the long term it would need to create a strong brand identity. It therefore enlisted the help of one of the largest advertising agencies in the US, TBWA/Chiat Day, to come up with a nationwide advertising campaign.

The campaign centred around a lovable sock puppet, designed to be a 'spokesdog' for the Pets.com brand. There was a great PR story about the creation of the sock puppet, which apparently involved putting together a six-page biography for the character. The adverts featured the puppet in a variety of different situations, such as flirting with housecats and protesting against socks being used as Christmas stockings. They also featured Pets.com's new strap line: 'Because Pets can't drive'. (No-one pointed out that most pets can't use computers either.) To ensure a maximum level of public awareness, the ads were aired during the Superbowl, the most contested and expensive of all advertising slots, as well as other commercial breaks with high audience figures.

The sock puppet became an overnight success. He appeared on *Good Morning America* and was interviewed by *People* magazine. He was floated down the streets of New York in Macy's Thanksgiving Day Parade and starred in his own line of licensed merchandise. By now he was more than a brand mascot, he was an A-list celebrity.

However, while the sock puppet had successfully caught the public's imagination, his popularity did not translate into sales. By the beginning of 2000, Pets.com was attracting fewer than a million visitors a month to its Web site.

The strategy of offering extreme discounts clearly wasn't working. According to Dan Janal, author of *Branding the Net*, the cost per customer acquisition for Pets.com was about US $80. 'There's no way you make that back when you sell a product with a paper-thin margin – and have ten other competitors doing the same.' But its discount policy wasn't Pets.com's only problem. It had also introduced free shipping – which was proving increasingly expensive for the company to sustain, especially when customers were ordering heavy bags of cat litter.

As with many other ill-fated dot.coms, Pets.com spent too much money on building awareness, and too little time questioning whether its Web site was a viable business in the long term. As a result, the company was spending over US $3.50 on marketing and sales expenses for every dollar it made in sales.

According to its many critics, Pets.com was too focused on 'going public' on the stock market, so that it could issue stock to investors in an initial public offering or IPO. As John Cassidy explains in *Dot.con*, Pets.com provides a classic example of how the Internet boom had inverted the traditional order of business:

> Instead of using the stock market to build companies, venture capitalists and entrepreneurs were now using companies to create stocks. Costly marketing campaigns were launched not only to attract customers but, more importantly, to grab the attention of potential shareholders. The task of building the company was secondary – a chore that had to be performed before the IPO.

Perhaps the main problem was that Internet users weren't ready to order their pet food online. Unlike Amazon, where customers could order rare titles they couldn't find in their local bookstore or record shop, Pets.com failed to offer real added value in terms of products. After all, dog food is dog food, and there clearly weren't enough people searching for ferret hammocks and other rare pet items that they wouldn't be able to find in their hometown. The only way the company could attract custom was to sell products below cost.

On 7 November 2000 Pets.com announced that it could no longer continue as a business, and as such became the first US dot.com on the stock market to close. In a statement made to the press on that same day, CEO Julie Wainwright explained the situation. 'It is well known that this is a very, very difficult environment for business-to-consumer Internet companies,' she said. 'With no better offers and avenues effectively exhausted, we felt that the best option was an orderly wind-down with the objective to try to return something to the stakeholders.'

Pets.com, as with boo.com, shows that a successful brand depends on a solid business plan. No matter how effective a company's advertising and PR proves to be, unless it can differentiate itself in terms of product and service and add real value, it will be left stranded.

There have also been some doubts about the effectiveness of the advertising in the first place. Andrea Reisman, CEO of Pets.com rival Petopia.com believed Pets.com was targeting the wrong people. 'We don't advertise on the Superbowl,' she said. 'That's not where our customer is.'

There is no denying that the adverts did have a lasting appeal though. Indeed, the sock puppets were among the most popular items sold on the Pets.com Web site. Ironically, the mascot used to build the brand had become bigger than the brand itself. Even after Pets.com had announced it was shutting up shop, interest in the sock puppet character was strong enough for him to be invited back on *Good Morning America*. Towards the end of the interview, the show's host asked the puppet if he had any advice for the investment community. And the puppet's response? 'Don't invest in dot.coms.'

Lessons from Pets.com

- *Differentiate your brand.* No market can support dozens of companies with similar business plans.

- *Add value.* 'In a product area where the retailer adds no extra value, Pets.com was doomed to disaster the day the first wave of competitors came along,' says e-marketing expert and author Dan Janal.
- *Don't compete on cost.* As discounts were the company's major selling point, Pets.com's profit margins eventually shrank to nothing.
- *Don't rely on gimmicks.* Sock puppets may be popular, but they can't single-handedly support a brand. Just ask ITV Digital.
- *Recognize that emotion isn't enough.* Pets.com vice president of marketing, John Hommeyer, was very proud of the bond the company had created with its customers. 'It's one of the few dotcoms that's really built a brand and established an emotional connection with consumers,' he said, shortly before the company's closure. When dealing with an online brand however, emotion isn't always enough to get consumers to buy online.
- *Have a strategy.* Pets.com's insufficient strategy was highlighted at the time by Michael Dunn, CEO of branding consultancy Prophet Brand Strategy. 'Most people have a playful, fun relationship with the sock puppet, but it has yet to translate into a compelling brand story that makes people want to transact with the company. Building a brand devoid of a clear business strategy is a recipe for failure.' And so it proved.

82 VoicePod

Failing to be heard

Technology company Altec Lansing learned the importance of marketing with its failed VoicePod digital recorder. As the leading maker of computer speakers, Altec was sure it had a hit on its hands with its innovative recorder that attached audio messages to e-mail.

PC World magazine said the VoicePod looked like 'a mouse on steroids – a lot of steroids – and promised to make your voice dramatically more helpful as a tool for the PC.' Gone, said Altec, are the days of unnecessary typing and fumbling for multimedia controls as its device offered the benefits of simple installation and use. VoicePod let users record and attach voice files to documents and e-mail messages with a few simple pushes of a button. There was another handy feature of the VoicePod: personal to-do lists. Users could dictate a short message to themselves and then save it.

The design was also technologically advanced as it exploited the company's 'signal processing technologies' that used noise removal filters and other technology to allow for minimum background noise and clear recording. 'With these features, the VoicePod could be a sound investment,' reckoned *PC World*. Not enough computer users agreed.

The trouble was, poor marketing had led to a lack of interest and aware- ness. The company was so confident that consumers would snatch the product off the shelves that it spent little money and effort on promotion. As a result sales were so poor that the company pulled the VoicePod from the market after just one month.

Lesson from Voice Pod

- *Don't ignore marketing.* 'Next time,' Altec president and CEO Mark Lucas told *Business 2.0* magazine at the time of the failure, 'we're making a huge marketing push.'

83 Excite@Home

Bad branding @ work

There was a time when Excite@Home was considered to be one of the 'safe bets' of the Internet revolution. Based around one simple service offering – the delivery of high-speed net access – investors were quick to see its potential. Then, bolstered by investment dollars, Excite@Home decided it wanted to be something bigger, and purchased a variety of online media properties including the Excite Web portal and Blue Mountain Arts in an attempt to build on AOL-style empire.

Although the company was once the leading cable Internet access provider, it fell behind the competition once it had broadened its ambitions. According to CNET journalist Ben Haskett, the demise of Excite@Home 'bordered on Greek tragedy,' with a history filled with tense boardroom skirmishes, ill-conceived acquisitions and executives who governed the operations from afar. 'Excite@Home was largely a victim of its own grandiose ambitions, as well as of a convoluted ownership structure that kept too many cooks in the kitchen,' Haskett wrote in his post-mortem of the company.

The merger of Excite and @Home (which was originally called just that) has been viewed as a critical mistake, although the motives were clear. William Hearst III, one of the Silicon Valley venture capitalists who helped to found the company, said:

> I felt the merger was a good idea at the time because I thought that when you're building a consumer marketplace, you need to have one-stop

shopping. One of the promises of the @Home idea was that you'd have a national brand, not a different brand in every marketplace. And as AOL has proven, if you have an e-mail product and a content product and a telecommunications product and a software product all under one single point of responsibility, you can build a very big company. That, I think, was the motive for the Excite merger: to build a company trying to produce a uniform consumer experience but on broadband instead of dial-up.

The merger didn't work though. Disputes between the telecom and media divisions meant that many management staff walked out. In addition, the company's CEO was running the business from Boston, more than 3,000 miles away from the Silicon Valley operation, which inevitably caused difficulties. It should also be noted that although Excite@Home offered cable Internet access, it offered this access over another company's cable lines, those of AT&T. Indeed, AT&T were the controlling shareholders, a fact which created further friction and conflicts of interest. For instance, according to Hearst, AT&T 'didn't share the content vision.' The problem was also one of timing. The dot.com collapsed once the company started to diversify. 'By the time the company decided to look at spinning off Excite, the marketplace had deteriorated,' explains Hearst. 'And meanwhile, the demand for broadband was growing so rapidly that the capital was needed to sustain the quality of service of the business.'

Perhaps the biggest problem, however, was marketing. Following the merger, Excite@Home simply wasn't able to differentiate itself or provide Internet users with a valid enough incentive to switch to their service. In January 2000 *Red Herring* magazine reflected:

Excite@Home hasn't exactly lived up to its name. Continual rotation of its advertising and messaging has sent this portal's brand identity into big-time obscurity. The company was on to something with its witty 'anyone can do it' TV campaign, but it disappeared in a blink. Yahoo is our whimsical guide; Infoseek our all-knowing soothsayer. Excite@ Home is more like a politician on the fence.

Lessons from Excite@Home

- *Avoid too many cooks.* Hearst says:

  One of the lessons is that you can gain a tremendous advantage by partnering with big, well-established companies, and people are going to continue to do that. But those companies are going to find it very difficult to put their new start-up venture ahead of their own corporate responsibilities. So when you have a start-up controlled by big, established companies, it's going to be a little different than a real, standalone start-up.

- *Don't over-reach.* Excite@Home's ambition to become the next AOL meant that it over-reached itself, spending money it couldn't afford.
- *Differentiate the brand.* Ultimately, consumers didn't have a clear idea of what the Excite@Home brand stood for. It meant everything and nothing, and as a result it failed.

84 WAP

Why another protocol?

In order to gain public awareness new technologies are now promoted as brands, by technological companies and organizations. However, often those technologies that receive the most hype die an early death while those that are launched with no fanfare gain mass acceptance.

Nowhere has this been more evident than with mobile phone technology. In Europe, the major mobile phone companies were unable to anticipate the success of SMS (short messaging service) text messaging. Indeed, some even failed to mention their phones included an SMS facility. As I explored in my previous book *Mobile Marketing*, mobile phone users were left to discover SMS for themselves – and discover it they did. In the UK alone, over 1 billion text messages are sent and received every single month.

In *Mobile Marketing*, I provided an overview of the technology's popularity:

> SMS, or the Short Messaging Service, was the first mainstream technology to enable short text messages to be sent from one mobile device to another. Devoid of colour, graphics, audio, video, and confined to 160 characters per message, SMS hardly seemed the most radical of new media technologies. Furthermore, people wanting to send an SMS text message had to work with small, fiddly mobile keypads and tiny grey screens.

Yet, for all its evident shortcomings, SMS became hugely popular and has inspired a whole generation of 'textheads', who have even conjured up their own SMS shorthand to overcome the character limit. Even among older users, SMS text messaging has proved to be a popular, less-intrusive and often cost-effective alternative to voice calls. While the mobile companies initially ignored this unassuming technology, they were very excited indeed about another three letter acronym: WAP.

WAP (wireless application protocol) was heralded as the first major global technology to make the mobile Internet a reality. And it was, although excessively slow download times and frequent connection failure along with many other usability shortcomings started to make people wonder if the wireless Web would be such a great thing anyway.

In 1999, the year WAP was being tweaked for launch in many countries, not a bad word could be found about this technology. Two years later headlines such as 'The Great WAP flop' and 'RIP WAP' were not uncommon in the European technology press.

One survey conducted in summer 2001 in the UK was especially telling. The BRMB study found that of the two-thirds of the population who owned a mobile phone, 85 per cent believed they had an SMS texting facility, while only 13 per cent said they had a WAP-enabled phone. Of that small number, only 37 per cent had used the WAP facility within the last month. Therefore most of those who were aware they were using a WAP device still didn't believe the WAP facility was worth using. As Simon Rogers commented in the *Guardian* at around the same time (July 2001) 'accessing a breaking news service using WAP just doesn't replicate the usefulness of the net and is little more than another incremental improvement on your phone.'

WAP's rough ride has been made even worse by the remarkable, and generally unpredicted, success of SMS. While WAP had been touted as a 'killer app' for wireless devices, the considerably less flashy SMS received little attention. When it suddenly emerged that in many parts of the world there were ten SMS users for every one WAP user, and that those SMS users were considerably more devoted than their weary WAP counterparts, it inevitably ruffled a few feathers.

The rumours regarding the death of WAP have been greatly exaggerated though as effective WAP applications have finally emerged. For most marketers however, WAP was something of a no-go area. *The Financial Times* has dubbed WAP marketing 'the least interesting type of wireless marketing.'

To be fair, many of the problems with WAP are not really its fault. After all WAP is only a protocol, and not a bad one at that. However, the term WAP has extended to encompass the entire mobile Internet experience via

WAP-enabled devices. And, up until now, that experience has been patchy to say the least.

As any brand strategist would agree, the success of a product or service depends not simply on its value, but rather its *perceived* value. So, whatever WAP will be able to offer mobile users in the future, the negative perception will take a while to erase. Even the WAP evangelists started to realize that it suffers from a certain public image problem. For instance, in 2002 the staunchly pro-WAP Web site WAPInsight (www.wapinsight.com) conceded that 'the signs are increasing that WAP as a brand name is dying'. The site reported the demise of the UK chain of retail stores run by MPC Telecom, called TheWAPStore, and said the 'WAP' element of the name sparked off negative associations among the public.

Whether WAP will disappear for good still remains to be seen and as more powerful mobile phones emerge the mobile Internet seems to have a positive future. However, the negative connotations of the WAP name means that a new acronym may have to be developed.

Lessons from WAP

- *Be useful.* WAP has suffered from a distinct lack of content mobile users could find useful on a WAP-based wireless Web. Although many companies have experimented with WAP sites, information *under*load remained a problem.
- *Be simple.* WAP has also suffered from comparisons with the more straightforward SMS. Unfavourable comparisons to Japanese I-mode technology have also added salt to WAP's wounds.
- *Don't overstate your case.* The initial WAP hype, which reached its hyperbolic peak in 1999–2000, overstated its case. One UK operator's campaign featuring a WAP-enabled surfboard, and many others like it, gave the impression of a mobile Internet 'surfer's paradise'. The protocol clearly couldn't deliver on this promise.
- *Be user-friendly.* Jakob Nielsen, ex-Sun Microsystems engineer and 'guru of Web usability' highlighted WAP's 'miserable usability'. In 2000, Nielsen advised businesses to 'skip the current generation of WAP'. Slow connections and downloads for the first wave of WAP meant that mobile users downloading WAP sites (particularly those with graphics) had a lot of spare time on their hands.

85 Dell's Web PC

Not quite a net gain

In late 1999, computer manufacturer Dell launched the Web PC. The computer was small (a mere ten inches in height) and came in five different colours. The aim of the computer was to simplify the experience of surfing the Internet, while at the same time being attractive. 'The quality of the customer's experience will be the defining source of loyalty in the Internet era,' Michael Dell told the press at the time. 'The Web PC is breaking new ground for our industry as we take our one-on-one relationships with customers to a new level of helpfulness.'

One of the key features of the product was an 'e-support button', that instantly launched a self-diagnostic programme. The button could also connect users directly to Dell's award-winning online technical support team.

The PC also included a 'sleep mode' designed to eliminate the time spent booting up the computer for Internet access. Users could simply push a button to instantly 'wake up' the computer.

'Many of these benefits are made possible by the 'legacy-free' design of the Web PC,' explained John Medica, the vice president and general manager of Dell's Web Products Group. 'We hand picked every piece of technology that went into the Web PC without carrying over any technology from previous PC designs that doesn't contribute to a pure Internet experience.'

The product was heavily marketed through a multi-media advertising campaign, centred around the slogan 'Born to Web', which drove customers to a Web PC Web site and free phone number, both of which acted as direct sales channels. In addition, Dell offered different peripheral products for the

Web PC, including such devices as a digital scanner, a joy stick and a digital camera.

The press heaped praise on the product, although most journalists saw it as an attempt to echo Apple's iMac strategy, with its emphasis on an eye-catching design, and user-friendly hardware. In his review for the *Washington Post*, Alan Kay said that although it 'focuses more on style than computing,' the Web PC is 'a decent PC that'll do most things you want.'

However, despite the number of benefits it offered, the Web PC was a flop. Dell pulled the machine from the market in June 2002, just six months after its release. Why? A number of reasons.

Firstly, the emphasis on design was misguided. Sure, the iMac had been a success. But Apple had always been about design, and Dell hadn't. Dell's core customers wanted good value and functionality, not groundbreaking design. Dell's Web PC was good-looking, but its looks were ultimately irrelevant. Whereas Dell usually uses its own in-house design team, for this project the company gave the job to a radical San Francisco-based design firm called Pentagram. 'I've designed great things that have been failures,' the chief designer told *Business 2.0* magazine. 'The product didn't fit what Dell is about.'

Computer User magazine noted another problem. 'Oddly, Dell is targeting its Web PC toward home or home-office markets where users would generally be better off with an expandable upgradeable system,' commented the reviewer. Dell's core market was traditionally business-orientated.

Then there was the price tag. Although it was billed as 'low cost', the price of US $999 was more expensive than many competing models. 'Consumers are looking at price first, then styling,' said Stephen Baker, a PC analyst at research firm PC Data. 'No-one aside from Apple has been able to crack that styling thing.'

Furthermore, Dell was selling in a completely new way. By offering a complete package, the world's number two computer maker was breaking with its typical practice of offering à la carte pricing that allows customers to mix-and-match computer chips and other components to create a customized PC. If the Dell brand signified anything it signified customization and functionality over design. The Web PC failed to offer either one of these values.

Lessons from Dell's Web PC

- *It's not about the product, it's about the brand.* The Web PC was not a bad product, as the plethora of positive reviews testifies. However, it did not fit well with the Dell brand.
- *A low-cost product needs to be perceived as such.* Although the Web PC was good value, because the price covered a complete package, it appeared too expensive.
- *Imitating the competition was a mistake.* When computer manufacturers saw the success of the iMac, they inevitably wanted a bite of the apple. This proved to be a misguided strategy for Dell, a company normally associated with 'beige and boxy' computers.

86 Intel's Pentium chip

Problem? What problem?

In 1997, a professor of mathematics found a glitch in Intel's Pentium chip. He discovered that the mathematical functions for the chip's complicated formula were not consistently accurate. The professor decided to send an article about his findings to a small academic newsgroup. Word spread through the university community and the editor of a trade title caught hold of the story. The general press then reported the professor's findings and sought Intel's response. Intel denied any major problem, declaring it would only affect a 'tiny percentage' of customers. They failed to take responsibility or replace the affected chips.

The issue grew online, as it became a key topic in an increasing number of online discussion groups, which kept on feeding the offline media. Intel's share value dropped by over 20 points. It was only when IBM's declaration that it would not use Intel chips in its computers made the front page of the *New York Times* that Intel went back on its previous position and agreed to replace the chips. Even today, evidence can be found of how Intel's poor response to online criticism has affected its reputation on the Net. The 'Intel Secrets' site at www.x86.org, which was set up at the time of the media's damning coverage of Intel's unhealthy chip, still emphasizes the faults to be found in various Intel products.

Lessons from Intel's Pentium chip

- *Remember that bad news makes the front page* – whereas good news is relegated to page 17 of the Sunday supplement; it's as simple as that. As Lord Northcliffe, the founder of the *Daily Mail*, once said: 'News is what somebody somewhere wants to suppress; all the rest is advertising.'
- *Don't ignore online criticism.* Alongside Intel, McDonald's, Shell, Apple, Netscape and, most frequently, Microsoft, have suffered as a result of letting negative issues develop online until the offline media pick them up and transform them into a crisis.
- *Respond quickly.* While the Internet may give people who have a grudge against your firm an attentive audience of similarly aggrieved individuals, it also gives businesses the opportunity to respond quickly and effectively to the spread of misinformation.
- *Monitor your critics.* Trouble builds-up slowly over time and, in all but the rarest cases, it is only poor management that transforms an 'issue' into a 'crisis'. Although cyberspace gives your e-critics a voice they may not have elsewhere, it also allows you to predict, locate and respond to negative publicity.

87 IBM's Linux graffiti

One of the best ways to generate publicity for a brand is to deploy unconventional tactics. For instance, when London nightclub the Ministry of Sound projected its logo onto the side of the Houses of Parliament, the media attention was immense. Indeed, it was considered such a successful trick that a few years later *FHM* promoted its '100 Sexiest Women of the Year' campaign with the same tactic, beaming the image of an almost naked Gail Porter (one of the contenders for the number one spot) onto the side of the historic building.

Such outlandish techniques are generally referred to as 'guerrilla marketing'. The logic behind guerrilla marketing is straightforward: if a company promotes itself in such a unique fashion it will not only be able to gain press coverage, but will also stick in people's minds and encourage word-of-mouth publicity. Furthermore, guerrilla marketing is usually cheap. When the online portal and search engine Yahoo! wanted to promote its Yahoo! mail services, it didn't decide to invest in hundreds of magazine ads. No. It built a couple of cows.

The company took part in an event called the Cow Parade in which cows were decorated according to different themes. Yahoo!'s 'udderly moovelous' (as it put it in a press release) pair of purple plastic cows were installed with an Internet facility that enabled members of the New York crowd to send 'moomail' messages to each other. Although this tactic was undeniably 'out there', it succeeded because it was relevant to the service it was promoting.

However, some guerrilla techniques have had considerably less success. For example, when IBM hired an innovative advertising agency to promote its Linux-based software, the campaign involved employing graffiti artists to scribble the words 'Peace, love and Linux' on pavements and walls through-out San Francisco and Chicago. Unfortunately, the bio-degradable chalk used to create the marketing messages turned out not to be so bio-degradable. Subsequently, IBM was charged with violation of city ordinance and had to pay a US $18,000 fine.

Lesson from IBM's Linux campaign

- *Think of the legal implications of any advertising campaign.* Marketers should plan and consider all repercussions for any campaign. After all, court appearances rarely help to positively boost a brand identity.

88 boo.com

The party's over

A magazine ad depicting a man vomiting into a dustbin may not be the most conventional tactic to use in order to sell sportswear, but then boo.com was hardly the most conventional company. The September 1999 advertising campaign, in which this image appeared, was designed to let everyone know that the first global sportswear site had arrived, in style, and that it was about to take the world by storm. Of course, the reality was rather different.

On 18 May 2000, less than a year after its launch, liquidators from the accounting firm KPMG were called in to the company's London head-quarters. After spending millions and attracting relatively few customers, boo.com became what *The Financial Times* referred to as 'the highest profile casualty among European e-tailing start-ups'.

Although boo.com is one of the most obvious and spectacular brand failures of the dot.com era – if not all time – it was founded on reasonably secure marketing logic. As Al and Laura Ries write in *The 22 Immutable Laws of Branding*, 'the most efficient, most productive, most useful aspect of branding is creating a new category.' There is no denying that ever since boo.com's Swedish founders Ernst Malmsten and Kajsa Leander had visited Amazon in 1997, they believed this was the key to dot.com success. As Malmsten writes in the best selling account of the boo phenomenon, *boo hoo*:

> If we were really to achieve the global impact we hoped for then we had
> to exploit 'first mover' advantage. If you're first, then you achieve vital

recognition as you become identified with whatever you're selling. You get a lot of free publicity and customer confidence because you're the leader. It's then very difficult for the second wave to compete. Amazon. com was a shining example of that. Here was a company that spent almost nothing on marketing before its IPO, but still managed to create one of the best known brands in the world.

When boo.com became public knowledge in May 1999, via an article in *The Financial Times*, Kasja Leander announced the company in these terms: 'Sportswear is an international market and there are a lot of people in Europe who read about products in US magazines but can't go over to buy them. This is one of the few sectors of Internet retailing that no one's done on a large scale and we want boo to be the number one brand.'

So neither Malmsten nor Leander can be accused of ignoring branding. The idea, from the start, was to create a 'fully branded shopping experience on the Net,' an online equivalent of high fashion department stores such as London's Harvey Nichols or New York's Bloomingdales, only with the main focus on urban and sportswear from hip brands such as Adidas, New Balance and North Face.

However, the brand that really mattered was boo itself. As Malmsten has explained, the aim was to make 'the name of the store itself as significant as anything you could buy in it.' Again, this displays solid brand-thinking, and marked boo apart from many other dot.coms that had sprung from the minds of technologists. But the problem was that whatever it can represent, the Internet *is* technology.

If you are going to create what Malmsten referred to as 'a gateway to world cool' (as quoted in a June 2000 *Industry Standard* article), you need software to make sure people can access the gateway in the first place. In other words, your Web site has to work.

On the first day of its eventual launch, 4 November 1999 (two months after the premature advertising campaign featuring the man vomiting into a dustbin) the problems with the boo.com Web site soon became apparent. The site crashed seconds after it went live. And then, when people could finally access the site, the real headaches, both for boo and its customers, began.

One of these headaches related to the heavy use of Flash software, which enabled the site to be animated. Indeed, one of the key features of the site was the virtual shop assistant Miss Boo who was only able to come to life through the use of Flash. However, many Internet users did not have a Web browser that could support this technology. Furthermore, in 1999 most PCs had a 56k (or slower) modem. This meant that the graphics-intensive site, which, as well as the attraction of Miss Boo offered visitors the chance to 'rotate' items before making a purchase, was going to be somewhat slow. How slow? Well, on an average computer the home page could take around three minutes to load and that was after having to sit through a lengthy animated introduction. Oh, and if you had a Mac you couldn't access the site at all.

Small wonder that the leading Internet usability experts, such as the high-profile author and Web engineer Jakob Nielsen, quickly pounced on boo. com as the archetypal example of how not to build a Web site. When he first reviewed the site for his Alertbox newsletter in December 1999, Nielsen could hardly believe what he saw:

> Instead of making it easy to shop, the site insists on getting in your face with a clumsy interface. It's as if the site is more intent on making you notice the design than on selling products. Furthermore, it is simply slow and unpleasant. All product information is squeezed into a tiny window, with only about one square inch allocated to the product description. Since most products require more text than would fit in this hole, boo requires the user to use a set of non-standard scroll widgets to expose the rest of the text. Getting to a product requires precise manipulation of hierarchical menus followed by pointing to minuscule icons and horizontal scrolling. Not nice.

Not nice indeed. But then, Alertbox was only distributed to 'techies', not the highly fashion-conscious affluent consumers boo wanted to reach. So why worry too much when they had already managed to secure complementary articles in the UK and US editions of *Vogue*, alongside various newspapers?

Ironically, the company founders' undeniable talent for publicity was starting to turn against them. Having spent millions on advertising and having generated thousands of column inches in the press, expectations had been inevitably high. While the company succeeded in creating a young and hip image (in 1999 *Fortune* magazine picked it as one of its 'Cool Companies' of the year) it had also placed itself under too bright a spotlight. Alongside attacks in the Internet media regarding the site's functionality – or rather, *lack* of functionality – the mainstream press was also starting to pick up on the parties and high living centred around the boo headquarters in London's Carnaby Street.

Malmsten now maintains that the company's extravagant reputation 'masked the reality' of the sheer amount of work that went on behind the scenes. Indeed, he reckons the 24/7 commitment his staff (or rather, 'boo crew') devoted to their task especially around the launch period, hadn't been seen since World War II. 'To understand this kind of total devotion to a cause you probably had to be in Britain in about 1940, when car factories were turning out aeroplanes or tanks overnight,' he writes in *boo hoo*, with no apparent trace of irony. But however hard everyone in the company was working in November 1999, the atmosphere had changed by the following February.

According to boo's financial strategist Heidi Fitzpatrick morale was low. 'We were out every lunchtime getting shit-faced. There was no management and we all went home at six instead of working all hours.' The reason for such low morale is represented by the figures. In a period of 18 months, the company had managed to get through approximately US $185 million that had been raised from high-profile investors such as Benetton, J P Morgan, Goldman Sachs, the French fashion conglomerate LVMH and the Lebanese Hariri family. How much of this money financed the first-class flights and Krug-swilling lifestyle boo was becoming increasingly famous for is impossible to say.

One thing, however, is for sure. There simply weren't enough customers. Deterred by a problematic Web site which concentrated on fancy design rather than straightforward product information, few people were willing to make the effort in any of the 18 countries where boo had a presence. In the first month after its November launch boo managed to sell around US $200,000 worth of stock, from which it profited half. Not bad by most e-commerce site's standards. But then, most e-commerce sites aren't capable of spending around US $20 million in a single month (as boo did that November). Although sales figures slowly increased, they weren't doing as quickly as boo had anticipated. Between February and April 2000, total sales were US $1.1 million. Unable to raise any more money from its investors, in May 2000 boo.com shut down and filed for bankruptcy.

In their final press release, one of the most famous statements of the dot.com era, Malmsten and Leander put their side of the story:

The senior management of boo.com has made strenuous efforts over the last few weeks to raise the additional funds that would have allowed the company to go forward with a clear plan. This plan involved a restructuring of the retail operations, the development of an e-fulfilment business using our unique advanced technology and operations platform, and the identification of strategic partners. It is disappointing to both the management and staff alike that we were not able to bring this plan to fruition against the background of steadily-improved trading.

The release concluded by stating: 'We believe very strongly that in boo.com there is a formula for a successful business.' Unfortunately, not everyone agreed. Among the many dissenters was Philip Kaplan, a 24-year-old New Yorker who launched FuckedCompany.com in 2000 to highlight what he referred to as the 'ridiculousness' of many dot.coms. The site quickly attracted hundreds of thousands of visitors, wanting to see which companies were next in line for the scrap-heap. When boo.com failed, Kaplan's response was, to say the least, cynical and his site put a rhetorical question to its visitors. 'Can you possibly think of anything that is a more eloquent testimony to having your head three feet up your Calvin-Klein-covered ass than to spend tens of million dollars on a dot.com start up AND NOT HAVE THE WEB SITE WORK?!'

There are others who take a kinder view though. Unlike the former staff at other doomed companies, many of the original boo team remain loyal to the memory and believe the company would have succeeded if only the investors had supplied more money.

It is also important to realize the wider context. When the news about boo's demise hit the headlines, the European dot.com community remained reasonably confident. This case was viewed as an isolated event, related only to the incompetence and extravagance within boo itself. The reality, however, was that boo.com's failure to survive was not unique. Only months after the front-page headline in *The Financial Times* 'Boo.com collapses as investors refuse funds', many others had suffered similar fates.

One of the journalists to have documented boo.com's ill-fortune was the BBC's Internet correspondent Rory Cellan-Jones. In his vivid account of dot.com Britain, *Dot.bomb*, he considers boo as part of a broader picture:

As other, less flamboyant companies also began to fail, it became clear that boo's problem was one of timing. Its vision of online retailing had won the support of investors, but neither the consumers nor the suppliers were yet ready to adopt it in significant numbers. When the investors lost faith in that vision, plenty of companies founded on the promise of the revolution were bound to fail. Boo simply got there first because it spent its money more quickly.

The medium was therefore becoming the message, and that message was increasingly one of failure. But boo's downfall cannot simply be attributed to the delusional late-1990s attitude towards the Internet which only hindsight has amended. Even if boo had been an offline company many of its mistakes would have been near-fatal. For instance, blowing millions of dollars on a risky launch campaign two months before the actual launch would always be a bad move.

Another mistake, ironically enough, could be put down to the company's obsession with the brand identity itself. The marketing people were often able to overrule the technical team, particularly with regard to crucial decisions regarding the Web site. As a result, the company created one of the most fabulous-looking sites on the Web, with the poorest functionality.

On the surface, boo was a great brand. But branding is about more than looking good. It is about fulfilling promises. The promises boo made – both to its investors and its customers – were ultimately undeliverable. And now boo's significance is not, as was intended, that of a global brand. Rather, through its negative example, it has helped us to learn the true value of the Internet for branding. It has highlighted the fact that whereas customers may require information and interaction, they want to access these benefits quickly and with minimal hassle.

That boo failed to realize that substance comes before style means that somebody, somewhere is probably still sitting at his or her computer waiting for the site's homepage to download.

Lessons from boo.com

- *Hire the right people.* 'The wrong people were hired – too many fresh faced consultants, too few wrinkled old retailers, and far too many warring factions,' says the BBC's Rory Cellan-Jones.

- *Understand the importance of timing.* A September launch campaign for a November launch was an inevitable waste of money.
- *Go for cost-effective marketing.* Towards the end of boo's lifespan the company promoted a money-off scheme. 'By far the most effective means of advertising the scheme turned out to be not expensive online banners or newspaper advertising by emails,' says boo co-founder Ernst Malmsten. This unsurprising realization came rather too late.
- *Make sure your Web site works.* With any Web site, particularly one with an e-commerce facility, it is best to go for a lowest common denominator approach. In other words, make sure it works on *every* customer's computer.
- *Appreciate that publicity works both ways.* If you put your brand under the media spotlight too early, every mistake you make will be noticed. Remember that publicity is good only when it is justified. Unless you can back it up with a solid brand performance it will turn against you.
- *Don't run a business with a crystal ball.* Running any business can be expensive, but if your sales figures are in the thousands, you probably shouldn't be spending millions in the hope that sales will improve in the future. Leave overly optimistic and unsupportable predictions to fortune-tellers and concentrate on the present reality.
- *Don't spread yourself too thin.* One of the main factors that contributed to boo's speedy demise was the decision to launch in 18 different countries simultaneously. A similar advertising campaign and identical Web site for each national market may have seemed like a good way to unify a global brand identity, but this costly and misguided strategy has subsequently become the archetypal 'how not to' example for businesses seeking to attract global audiences.

CHAPTER 10

Tired brands

All brands will eventually fail. There is no such thing as a brand that can last forever. Some go out with a bang, others with a pitiful whimper, but they will all, at some stage, come face to face with their own mortality.

But what about Coca-Cola? What about McDonald's? Well, they are unlikely to disappear tomorrow, or even in the next few decades, but is it really impossible to imagine some future, more health-conscious society rejecting these in favour of brands more in tune with the age?

Many of the strongest brands of the last century are starting to look very tired. Many more have already failed. This chapter is therefore devoted to formerly successful brands, which are either no longer with us, or are looking gradually weaker day by day.

89 Oldsmobile

How the 'King of Chrome' ended up on the scrap heap

Oldsmobile is among the brand legends in US car history. Conceived in 1897, it was one of the five core brands manufactured by General Motors (GM) – the other four being Chevrolet, Pontiac, Buick and Cadillac – and helped lead the company to a 57 per cent share of the US car market by the middle of the last century.

For decades, Oldsmobile was a pioneering brand. In the 1920s, it became known as the 'King of Chrome' because it was the first car with chrome-plated trim. A decade later it became the first production line car in the US with a fully automatic transmission. In 1966, it introduced a car with front wheel drive.

However, in more recent times Oldsmobile has lost its pioneering edge. GM famously decided that instead of preserving and accentuating the unique identity of each of its brands it would increase its profits 'through uniformity'. As a result, Oldsmobiles began to look very similar to other GM cars, with only small, superficial differences.

In 1983 a *Fortune* magazine article highlighted the growing homogeny of the GM brands by including a photograph of an Oldsmobile alongside a Chevrolet, a Buick and a Pontiac. The article's headline was, 'Will Success Spoil General Motors?', but it may as well have been, 'Spot the Difference'. The article described GM's new state-of-the-art assembly plant at Orion, Michigan:

The $600-million plant bristles with robots, computer terminals, and automated welding equipment, including two massive $1.5 million Ploogate systems that align and weld assemblies of body panels. Unmanned forklifts, guided by wires buried in the floor, will carry parts directly from loading docks. In its flexibility, Orion sets new standards for GM plants.

But while GM's technology may have been cutting edge, the values associated with the Oldsmobile brands were anything but. An article in the *Detroit News* in May 2002 explained the problem the Detroit-based company faced in the 1980s and 1990s:

GM's historic brand strategy, pioneered by chairman Alfred Sloan in the 1920s, counted on consumers methodically moving up the ladder of affluence from Chevrolet to Buick to Oldsmobile to Cadillac. The game plan worked when GM built distinct cars for every division, but fell apart when the company slapped different nameplates on essentially the same vehicles. A solid, but staid Oldsmobile has little appeal to consumers enamoured with sleek Audi sedans or Toyota's elegant Lexus luxury cars.

Loyalty, instead of enthusiasm, drew consumers to GM showrooms. The average age of owners of Oldsmobile, Buick and Cadillac drifted into the mid-60s.

Towards the end of the 1990s, GM unveiled a new branding strategy to combat this lack of enthusiasm. The idea was to focus more on specific models rather than the brand division. Within the Oldsmobile range, GM launched the Alero, Aurora and Intrigue models in an attempt to catch up with its slicker rivals. Although the new cars received various positive reviews within the automotive press, and an intensive marketing drive that included strategic appearances in *The X-Files*, they failed to capture the share of the younger market they were designed to attract.

At the end of 2000, GM made what must have been a painful, if unavoidable decision to gradually phase out the Oldsmobile brand. The Oldsmobile collector's models mark the end of production. From 2004, no future Oldsmobile models will be manufactured.

Since the decision was made, marketing experts have been conducting post-mortems of the brand to see what exactly went wrong. One mistake that has been highlighted repeatedly is GM's attempt to strip the brand of its old-fashioned connotations. This was always going to be difficult for a car that predates Ford and even has the word 'old' within its name.

GM tried to get round this problem by launching an advertising campaign based around the slogan, 'This is not your father's Oldsmobile'. However, as Coca-Cola discovered with New Coke, it is not easy to reverse a brand identity which has been a century in the making. Another, rather pointless tactic was to build Oldsmobiles without the name Oldsmobile on the outside of the car. One *Brand Week* article, published in February 2001 after GM made its decision public, examines the folly of such branding exercises:

> The problem [Oldsmobile] encountered is that brands, particularly brands with a well-established image, cannot be repositioned. At best they may be nudged slowly in a new direction but not one that is the antithesis of what it stood for [. . .] A better solution, and a more unique approach, would have been to accept the brand as it was, with its older profile, and give its older customers a product they wanted to own with a message that appealed to their needs. In addition to capitalising on the existing profile of the brand, that strategy would have taken advantage of the growing number of mature Americans and their increased spending power.

The Oldsmobile hadn't always been viewed as staid and boring though. Although it had never been a youth brand, it had been considered an innovator in its field. The most critical brand damage therefore occurred when this reputation faded, and the motivation to buy an Oldsmobile (as opposed to another GM car) no longer remained so great.

However, despite these obvious failings, affection among Oldsmobile's traditional customers is still strong. There is even a Web site (www.saveolds mobile.org) dedicated to encouraging GM to reverse its decision to phase the brand out. But a visit to the Web site will only serve to remind you that the significance of the Oldsmobile brand is confined to the past. The affection most feel for the car is already tinged with nostalgia. Indeed, if it is the job of branding to distinguish one product from the next in the mind of the customer, the Oldsmobile brand failed decades ago.

Lessons from Oldsmobile

- *Make your brand distinctive.* When GM decided to adopt a policy of uniformity, the Oldsmobile brand became too, well, general.
- *Don't betray your brand values.* 'One can change some of the elements providing that the consumer continues to recognise that the same brand values are still present after the change,' says Jacques Cherron of brand consultancy JRC&A. Attempting to convert Oldsmobile into a young and hip brand was clearly one brand betrayal too far.

90 Pear's Soap

Failing to hit the present taste

Pear's Soap was not, by most accounts, a conventional brand failure. Indeed, it was one of the longest-running brands in marketing history.

The soap was named after London hairdresser Andrew Pears, who patented its transparent design in 1789. During the reign of Queen Victoria, Pear's Soap became one of the first products in the UK to gain a coherent brand identity through intensive advertising. Indeed, the man behind Pear's Soap's early promotional efforts, Thomas J Barratt, has often been referred to as 'the father of modern advertising.'

Endorsements were used to promote the brand. For instance, Sir Erasmus Wilson, President of the Royal College of Surgeons, guaranteed that Pear's Soap possessed 'the properties of an efficient yet mild detergent without any of the objectionable properties of ordinary soaps.'

Barrat also helped Pear's Soap break into the US market by getting the hugely influencial religious leader Henry Ward Beecher to equate cleanliness, and Pear's particularly, with Godliness. Once this had been achieved Barratt bought the entire front page of the *New York Herald* in order to show off this incredible testimonial.

The 'Bubbles' campaign, featuring an illustration of a baby boy bathed in bubbles, was particularly successful and established Pear's as a part of everyday life on both sides of the Atlantic. However, Barratt recognized the ever changing nature of marketing. 'Tastes change, fashions change, and the advertiser has to change with them,' the Pear's advertising man said in a 1907 interview. 'An idea that was effective a generation ago would fall flat, stale, and unprofitable if presented to the public today. Not that the idea of today is always better than the older idea, but it is different – it hits the present taste.'

Throughout the first half of the 20th century, Pear's remained the leading soap brand in the UK. However, towards the end of the century the market was starting to radically evolve.

In an October 2001 article in the *Guardian*, Madeleine Bunting charted our love affair with soap:

> Over the past 100 years, soap has reflected the development of consumer culture. Some of the earliest brand names were given to soap; it was one of the first mass-produced goods to be packaged and the subject of some of the earliest ad campaigns. Its manufacturers pioneered market research; the first TV ads were for soap; soap operas, tales of domestic melodrama, were so named because they were often sponsored by soap companies. Soap made men rich – William Hesketh Lever, the 33-year-old who built Port Sunlight [where Pear's was produced], for one – and it is no coincidence that two of the world's oldest and biggest multinationals, Unilever and Procter & Gamble, rose to power on the back of soap.

Recently though, Bunting argued, a change has emerged. The mass-produced block has been abandoned for its liquid versions – shower gels, body washes and liquid soap dispensers. 'In pursuit of our ideal of cleanliness, the soap bar has been deemed unhygienic,' she claimed.

Of course, this was troubling news for the Pear's Soap brand and, by the end of the last century, its market share of the soap market had dropped to a low of 3 per cent. Marketing fell to almost zero. Then came the fatal blow. On 22 February 2000 parent company Unilever announced it was to discontinue the Pear's brand. The cost-saving decision was part of a broader strategy by Unilever to concentrate on 400 'power' brands and to terminate the other 1,200. Other brands for the chop included Radion washing powder and Harmony hairspray.

So why had Pear's lost its power? Well, the shift towards liquid soaps and shower gels was certainly a factor. But Unilever held onto Dove, another soap bar brand, which still fares exceptionally well. Ultimately, Pear's was a brand built on advertising and when that advertising support was taken away, the brand identity gradually became irrelevant. After years of staying ahead, Pear's Soap had failed to 'hit the present taste' as Thomas J Barratt might have put it.

Lessons from Pear's

- *Every brand has its time*. Pear's Soap was a historical success, but the product became incompatible with contemporary trends and tastes.
- *Advertising can help build a brand*. But brands built on advertising generally need advertising to sustain them.

91 Ovaltine

When a brand falls asleep

In 2002, the Ovaltine brand celebrated its 98th birthday. That same year, it closed its UK factory and was forced to admit it had finally lost its main market. The Ovaltine brand was put up for sale and, at the time of writing, no interested buyers have emerged.

First produced by a Swiss food company in 1904, the malt drink with added vitamins became the UK's favourite bedtime drink. However, although commonly sipped to get a good night's sleep, the original advertising for the brand highlighted opposite qualities. Indeed, Ovaltine was an official sponsor of the 1948 Olympics and was billed as an 'energy drink' years before the term became widely adopted. In 1953, it was used by Sir Edmund Hillary on his famous Everest expedition and it was even reported to cure impotence, decades before the arrival of Viagra.

Curiously, this image was reversed in the later 20th century, and it became more popular as a cure for insomnia than a tonic for athletes and the sexually challenged. As Mark Lawson wrote in the *Guardian* in June 2002, it also became seen as a drink for the elderly through advertising campaigns steeped in nostalgia:

> The singing kiddies of the radio show, winsome in their Winceyette pyjamas, were accurate reflections of contemporary childhood at the time they started but, as they continued to be the official faces of the brand, kept sending the subliminal image that it was something your

granny used to drink. In common with cocoa and Horlicks, Ovaltine took on the image of the sedative nightcap of veterans. Any potential buyer for the drink might reflect that the backwards-looking website Sterling Time – dedicated to 'British nostalgia. . . Englishness and patriotism' – contains a large section memorialising the Ovaltineys [the children used for the 1930s Ovaltine campaigns].

Future anthropologists may also be interested in the fact that so many people were once drawn to draughts reputed to put you out for the night. Part of the reason for the decline of Ovaltine is surely that more recent generations exist in a habitual state of exhaustion, caused by longer working hours, the collapse of public transport and the cult of intensive, hands-on parenting among young mums and dads. They are also far more likely than their grandparents to drink wine nightly and have the option of late-night or all-night television: all reliable knockouts. Graham Norton, Jacob's Creek and long-distance commuting now achieve much of what Ovaltine used to.

When Ovaltine sales started to slip, it launched spin offs such as Chocolate Ovaltine, Ovaltine Light and Ovaltine Power. It also started to use contemporary children in its advertising, in its attempt to reposition itself as a 'now brand' as opposed to a 'then brand'.

However, unlike other drink brands – such as Lucozade, which moved from medicine status to sporty essential through clever marketing – Ovaltine has not been able to shake off its sleepy, nostalgic identity. Whether a new owner will be able to perform such a miracle remains to be seen.

Lessons from Ovaltine

- *Don't build unpopular brand associations.* 'The problem of this traditional bedtime cuppa is that it had become associated with two unpopular commodities, nostalgia and somnolence,' wrote Mark Lawson.
- *Don't fall into the nostalgia trap.* Nostalgia can be a powerful selling force, but it can also ultimately make a brand irrelevant to the present market.

92 Kodak

Failing to stay ahead

Can a brand become too successful? The short answer, of course, is no it cannot. Is it possible to conceive that the success and popularity of a brand such as Coca-Cola or McDonald's could become a weakness? Surely not. And yet, the strongest brands are also those which are the most tied down. Consumers know what they want from Coca-Cola (cola) and McDonald's (fast food) and they don't want anything different. If McDonald's wanted to set up a vegetarian, high class restaurant, it would need to change its brand name in order to attract customers. Coca-Cola has learnt this lesson from real experience. When it launched a range of Coca-Cola clothes, sales were far lower than had been expected. The trouble was, although Coca-Cola is an internationally adored brand, people don't want to *wear* it, they'd prefer to *drink* it.

So to ask the question again, can a brand become too successful? No, providing the brand stays within the same product category. If a brand becomes globally associated with one type of product, it is almost impossible to change the consumer's perception. After all, brands are *names*. If two people have exactly the same name it can become confusing, and so it is with products. But what if the product category itself changes, regardless of the brand's will? This situation may never have affected Coca-Cola or McDonald's, as there will always be demand for cola and fast food, but it has affected others, most notably Kodak.

Perhaps no market in the world is currently changing with more speed than photography. More and more consumers are trading their standard photographic cameras for digital alternatives. Many experts have predicted that it is only a matter of time before the entire camera market goes digital.

Kodak, however, is a name intrinsically associated with conventional photographs. When most people think Kodak, they think little yellow boxes of film. They don't think cutting-edge digital technology.

According to Harvard Business School professor John Kotler, the market shift towards digital photography constitutes 'a howling, horrifically difficult challenge' for the brand. 'For a century Kodak had too much success and too much market share. It was as bad as IBM at its worst.'

How has Kodak responded to this challenge? It entered the digital arena in 1995 with the creation of the Kodak Digital Science brand. However, the following year saw the company invest heavily in conventional photography with the development of the Advanced Photo System (branded as the Kodak Advantix system). This new system offered various advantages for the consumer, including a choice of three print formats.

However, the development of the Advantix cameras and films was extremely expensive for Kodak. Between 1996 and 1998 the company invested US $200 million in the system, only to discover it had distribution problems. Not enough retailers were interested in stocking the cameras and films, and there were not enough places where the Advantix films could get processed.

Some brand commentators, including Al Ries and Jack Trout, have questioned the logic behind the decision to invest so heavily in conventional photography – albeit *advanced* conventional photography – at a time when the market was starting to head towards digital photography. 'Wouldn't it be better to let the old system die a natural death and use the money to build a new digital brand?' Ries asks, rhetorically, in *The 22 Immutable Laws of Branding*.

Kodak stuck with Advantix though, and its persistence paid off, at least in the short term. By 1997 its Advantix product range accounted for 20 per cent of all Kodak sales. However, it looks unlikely that Advantix will be enough to stop photography customers 'going digital'. And the investment in the Advantix system has only served to reaffirm the association with conventional photography. Even now, too few consumers are familiar with the Kodak Digital Science brand. As Des Dearlove and Stuart Crainer explain in *The Ultimate Book of Business Brands*, the company needs to change its competitive strategy if the brand is to survive in the long term: 'Today, Kodak is competing not just with arch rival Fuji but with hungry Silicon Valley predators in search of a share of the emerging digital-photo market. The challenge facing the company is to transform itself into a high-performing organization, capable of holding its own with the likes of Canon and Microsoft'.

However, the Kodak brand has been tied with conventional photographic film since it was introduced in 1885, and the reputation will be hard to change. Furthermore, numerous other photography brands have a broader, more digital-friendly reputation. Not only Canon, but Minolta, Sharp, Sony, Casio and many more.

Furthermore, every time a technology makes a major advance, entirely new brands emerge on the scene. When the home computing market exploded, along came Apple. When mobile phone technology took off, along came Orange. Kodak itself was once a pioneering new brand for a pioneering new technology, famously promoted with the slogan 'You push the button – we do the rest'. Now though, the brand name carries with it over a century's worth of brand perceptions which are out of sync with the digital era. The question Kodak executives will resist, but ultimately may have to face, is whether it is time to push the button on the brand itself.

Opinions from the marketing experts are divided. Dearlove and Crainer believe its former successes will be enough to carry the brand through claiming, 'the Kodak brand is likely to survive in one form or another – it is too valuable to be allowed to die.' Ries, on the other hand, believes Kodak doesn't stand a chance: 'The Kodak brand has no power beyond the realm of conventional photography.'

If Kodak is to stand a fighting chance it needs to make some tough and potentially risky decisions. It will find it increasingly hard to keep one foot in conventional photography and the other in digital. After all brands are built on 'either/or' rather than 'both/and' policies.

As branding is a process of differentiation, Kodak must still preserve a unique identity in order to stand out from its competitors. At the same time, it must be able to form a brand image that is as cutting-edge as the technology it is starting to promote. This is by no means impossible. After all, providing photography survives in some form Kodak will have a fighting chance. Its strategic partnership with AOL for its 'You've got Pictures' service was certainly a move in the right direction.

It will, however, mean making some tough and difficult decisions. Among these will be the most difficult decision a brand ever had to make: should it divorce itself from its own heritage? Although difficult, it is better that this decision is made by the brand on its own accord, rather than forced upon it at a later date by the state of the market. Whether it will be possible is another question entirely, and only time will tell. Ultimately, Kodak may be forced to create a new brand altogether.

Lessons from Kodak

- *Markets do not stay static*. Markets are always in a constant state of flux, especially those which are based around technology.
- *Brands have a lifespan*. The Kodak brand has been around since the 1880s, making it one of the oldest technology brands in existence. Now, the brand may be reaching the end. 'There is a time to invest in a brand and there is a time to harvest a brand,' says Ries. 'And, ultimately, there is a time to put the brand to sleep.'
- *Success is a double-edged sword*. The more successful a brand becomes within one market, the more difficult it becomes for the brand to adapt when that market changes.

93 Polaroid

Live by the category, die by the category

If digital photography represents a difficult challenge for Kodak, it represented a near impossible one for Polaroid. In October 2001, after years of falling sales and drastic cost cuts, the firm filed for bankruptcy. Although the company was eventually purchased in July 2002 by the private equity arm of Bank One, many believe the glory days of Polaroid are in the past.

However, digital cameras are only one contributing factor in the perceived decline of the instant photography brand. To understand how it was unable to maintain its once formidably strong brand assets, it is necessary to understand how the brand evolved.

Polaroid was founded by Harvard graduate Edwin Land in 1937, who had spent years researching ways to reduce the problem of glare within photographs. Indeed, early Polaroid products included glare-reducing desk lamps and eye glasses.

In the years after World War II, Polaroid became chiefly associated with instant photography. Land, who had pioneered a process in which coloured dyes were able to be passed from a negative onto film inside a sealed unit, launched his first camera in 1948 and by the 1970s the brand was a household name. In fact, as the first and only brand within its category, the brand became the name of the end product itself. In other words, people didn't say 'a Polaroid photograph' or even 'a photograph', they simply said 'a Polaroid'.

Polaroid's profile was enhanced further during the 1970s through the long-running advertising campaign for the company's One Step camera, featuring actors James Garner and Mariette Hartley in romantic roles. Because of its instantaneous nature, with photos developed in your hand seconds after they were taken, the Polaroid identity became that of a fun, cool 'live for the moment' kind of brand.

The 1970s also saw Polaroid develop an almost cult status, with various high-profile figures becoming passionate fans of the brand. The art world, in particular, became a fan of instant photography. This was no accident. Edwin Land had understood that artists could help to legitimize his invention since the 1950s. He had known that if Polaroid was seen as a novelty, or a gimmick, the brand would die as quickly as it had emerged. He therefore needed to establish Polaroid photography as a potential art form in its own right.

In 1955 he had found the solution in the form of Ansel Adams, an internationally acclaimed landscape photographer who had exhibited at the Museum of Modern Art in New York. Adams was sent out to Yosemite National Park in California to experiment with different types of Polaroid film. Artistic photographs of snow-covered landscapes which rivalled much of Adams former work were the end result. With the help of a 'serious' photographer such as Adams, Polaroid was now a brand to be treated with respect. Such was this success that every time Land created a new film he would invite photographers and artists to the Polaroid labs to see what they thought. There is even an official Polaroid Collection of Art which has been lovingly built up and now includes over 20,000 works.

By the mid 1970s, modern artists of a very different nature to Ansel Adams became Polaroid devotees. Such luminaries as Andy Warhol, David Hockney, William Wegman, Chuck Close, Lucas Samaras and Marie Cosindas were all big fans. Warhol, in particular, loved his Polaroid camera. He had it with him at all times and snapped everyone he met on his hedonistic adventures around Manhattan.

In an article which appeared in the *Guardian* in October 2001, Jonathan Jones explained the connection between the Polaroid brand and the art world:

> Polaroid colour is intense, slightly unreal, adding its own sheen to an image. This appealed to artists because it made explicit the artifice of the photographic [. . .] The revolution that made Polaroid a universal tool for artists, as well as a truly mass photographic method, was the

launch of its SX-70 camera in 1972. This was the first camera to have an integral Polaroid film, so you took the picture and saw it come out of the camera in an instant.

Since the company became a household name in the early 1970s, Polaroid had been used by artists to make dirty, cheap, quick, casual pictures whose contribution to the good name of Polaroid is debatable [. . .] The 1970s were the golden age of the Polaroid, but not in a way that lived up to Land's artistic ideals.

In other words, the endorsement of artists and photographers which Land had so craved was now having a counterproductive impact on a brand seeking to establish instant photography as a serious medium. So while Polaroid's popularity continued to rise, in many ways its credibility started to diminish.

With Polaroid viewed as a fun, frivolous and even throwaway brand, consumers rarely considered a Polaroid as a substitute for a 'normal' camera. These cameras were usually seen as a luxurious and optional product, which although they might provide fun at parties, would never be as good as a Canon for taking family portraits.

This problem could have been partially resolved if 'conventional' photography brands such as Kodak were seen by the public to be treating instant photography seriously. In fact, Kodak *had* treated it seriously and planned to compete against Polaroid with its own range of instant cameras. Polaroid, however, was unwilling to share its market with anyone else and filed a lawsuit against Kodak. But while Polaroid may have won in the courts, it had effectively stopped the growth of the instant photography market.

This deliberate strategy of isolation was to cause further problems in the 1980s when more affordable conventional 35mm cameras saturated the US market, assisted by the emergence of one-hour photo shops. Customers could get high quality photos without waiting a week for them to be developed. This meant that Polaroid was gradually losing its key brand asset. It hadn't been able to compete on quality for some time, but it had been able to compete on speed. Now even that was being taken away.

The final blow was the arrival en masse of home computers and digital cameras. In his account of Polaroid's demise, BBC News Online's North America business reporter neatly summed up the superiority of digital photography: 'Not only could pictures be taken and viewed instantly, but they could be sent hundreds if not thousands of miles away with a mere click or two of a computer mouse.'

Rapidly, the Polaroid brand was running out of options. It had already tried to expand into conventional 35mm photographic film, but had failed to convert enough Kodak customers. The brand association of Polaroid and instant photography had proven too strong in consumers' minds. Polaroid proved equally incapable of turning itself into a digital-imaging company. This surprised many analysts who believed Polaroid would have a better chance than Kodak had in competing within the digital arena. 'Nobody was in a better position than Polaroid to capitalise on digital photography,' said Peter Post, CEO of Cossette Post, a part of Canada's largest marketing company, Cossette Communications Group. 'What's a bigger benefit than its instantaneous nature? Polaroid could have been a major force in digital photography today if somebody had looked out into the culture and tried to figure out where the brand would fit in. They just never went there.'

Ironically, for a brand associated with speed and instantaneity, one of the major criticisms levelled against Polaroid was that it was too slow in reacting to changes in the market. It had failed to anticipate the implications of digital photography, just as it had been unable to respond effectively to the rise in one-hour photo shops a decade before.

The creativity that Edwin Land had displayed when building his company simply wasn't there anymore. As the famous US entrepreneur David Oreck stated in a lecture on 'Who's Killing America's Prized Brand Names?' there is a dangerous trend against creativity within many long-established companies. 'Business managers are averse to risk. Wall Street people don't want risks; they want this quarter's results. But the visionary has a higher respect for the brand. We have to find a way not to stifle the creative person,' he said. 'There's still more poetry than science in business.'

Another failing attributed to the Polaroid brand is that it is a 'one-trick pony'. It fought to become the one and only name in instant photography and has now paid the price. Yet brands *can* evolve. If Polaroid had been clever it could have branded digital products as a logical and even inevitable extension of its instant photography range.

Other experts have concluded that Polaroid should have concentrated less on the specific products it made and more on the particular values it represented to the consumer. Even John Hegarty, the chairman of Polaroid's advertising agency, joined in this attack. 'Polaroid's problem,' he diagnosed, 'was that they kept thinking of themselves as a camera. But the "[brand] vision" process taught us something: Polaroid is not a camera – it's a social lubricant.'

If Polaroid had concentrated on the unique 'sociable' aspects of the brand, rather than the unique technological aspects, it would have certainly been less vulnerable when technology overtook its core product offerings. But by the end of the 1990s it had left it too late. Debts were mounting, and the brand was by that point associated with the Polaroid camera. The terrorist attacks of 11 September 2001 caused a slowdown in travel, and consequently a decline in demand for cameras and films. These bleaker market conditions proved too much. By that time Polaroid had amassed debts of almost US $1 billion, and the company's share value slipped from a high of US $60 in 1997 to a low of 28 cents in October 2001. That same month, the company filed for bankruptcy.

Lessons from Polaroid

- *Be quick.* Polaroid was slow to anticipate and respond to future trends, such as digital photography and one-hour photo shops.
- *Don't be over-protective.* In forcing Kodak out of instant photography, Polaroid was defending its brand at the expense of the market. Very few brands can sustain a product category single-handedly over the long-term. Polaroid therefore went against 'The Law of the Category' as formulated by Al and Laura Ries. Namely, that 'leading brands should promote the category, not the brand.'
- *Focus on values, not products.* According to Kevin Roberts, the US chief executive of Saatchi and Saatchi, for a brand to be truly successful it needs to become a 'lovemark' rather than a 'trademark'. In other words, the brand needs to inspire passion. Roberts cites Coca-Cola, Nike and Harley Davidson as classic lovemarks. In order to create a lovemark, Polaroid would have needed to focus on its value as a 'social lubricant' (to borrow John Hegarty's phrase). This would have helped to increase Polaroid's elasticity (see below).
- *Be elastic.* Branding author Jack Trout observed that companies are limited to one idea per brand. When that idea is the product itself, as opposed to the values it represents, brands become inflexible.

- *Feel it, don't fight it.* Polaroid's early brand vision was to establish instant photography as a serious artistic medium. However, by the 1970s this vision was undermined by pop artists who loved its fun and frivolous associations. Polaroid resisted this image for too long, just as it resisted other external factors that impacted on the brand.

- *Stay relevant.* 'Brands that don't keep up can get lost quickly,' says Peter Post of Canadian marketing firm Cosette Post in a brandchannel.com article by John Kavolefski. 'They first become irrelevant, then invisible, and then they're gone.' Instead of exploiting the opportunity offered by digital photography, Polaroid was concentrating on developing a 35mm colour print film.

- *Stay creative.* 'A lot of these older brands start to lose any kind of creativity in their strategic thinking,' says marketing consultant, Bruce Tait in the brandchannel.com article. 'The whole idea should be to insert originality into the strategic process, and push to be relevant and differentiated. There's too much belief in marketing as a scientific process. People have too few ideas. The leads to sameness in strategy and that's why brands die.'

- *Be essential.* With the arrival of digital photography there is no longer a *need* for Polaroid's style of instant photography. For instance, whereas building site managers used to rely on Polaroid in their professional life, they now use digital cameras to take on-site pictures. The only exception is in the legal field, as Polaroid film remains the only thing certain courts accept as evidence because it cannot be altered.

94 Rover

A dog of a brand

Rover has been making cars since 1904 and contributed its share of technological advances – the Rover gas turbine car in 1950 and the four-wheel drive T3 in 1956 with its fibreglass bodywork.

The P4, P5 and P6 series became hallmarks of British motoring throughout the 1960s and 1970s, with the P4 affectionately known as 'Auntie' Rover. During the prosperous post-war years, Britons bought as many Rovers as the company could turn out, but its industrial problems in the 1970s signalled the start of a long decline.

In 1994 BMW bought the UK manufacturer, trying to transform it into a competitive carmaker for the 21st century. But BMW was mainly interested in the group's Land Rover division of four-wheel drive vehicles.

The Rover 75 was the first new car produced after BMW had bought the troubled company so every effort was made to ensure that it was a technical and aesthetic success. At first, these efforts seemed to have paid off. Across Europe, Japan and the Middle East, the Rover 75 was heralded as an excellent car by the automotive press during the year of its launch, 1999. One magazine commended its 'elegant retro look', and described it as 'classy, stylish and refined.' In total, the car won 10 international motor industry awards. And yet, despite such weighty endorsements, people have been reluctant to buy the car. In 1999, just 25,000 were sold, which was well below target figures.

The problem, it appeared, was not with the car itself, but with the brand. According to Jeremy Clarkson the Rover name has a certain stigma attached to it. 'It's just about the least cool badge in the business,' he said. 'Rover, the name, is a dog.'

Of course, this may only be a matter of opinion. The sales figures, on the other hand, are a matter of fact. 'A look at the numbers shows that the buyers are bargain hunters who flock to the showrooms only in response to extra-ordinary discounts,' reported the BBC. The sluggish sales associated with the Rover 75 were therefore symptomatic of a broader problem regarding the Rover name itself. The company had become, in the words of one journalist, 'a living symbol of the UK motor industry's decline.'

'The Rover 75 was the turning point. It was supposed to be the car that set the seal on Rover's renaissance,' says Jay Nagley of the Spyder consultancy. 'The Rover 75 was a good car, but the problem with Rover is the image. People in that market sector didn't necessarily want the Rover image no matter how good a car it was attached to.'

By March 2000, BMW had had enough. With Rover piling up £2m losses a day, the firm decided to break up the company.

Lessons from Rover

- *If the name doesn't work, change it.* Critics suggested the Rover name should be dumped and rebranded as Triumph.
- *Concentrate on the brand not the products.* 'The problem is the brand rather than the cars,' said motor consultant Jay Nagley.

95 Moulinex

Going up in smoke

Moulinex, the French-based electrical household appliance manufacturer, filed for bankruptcy in September 2001. The action placed the brand in immediate jeopardy, but was seen as necessary. 'If they want to keep going but the shareholders wouldn't agree, they had to do this, otherwise it would have meant liquidation,' said one analyst at a Paris-based brokerage.

As the company neared collapse, Moulinex's 21,000 employees started to resort to unusual methods in order to keep their jobs. One microwave factory in northern France was occupied by workers and then set on fire. The following day employees returned and threatened to detonate homemade bombs to destroy what was left of the plant. According to *Business Week* magazine, union officials even kidnapped the government appointed mediator to try and get a better deal on lay-off packages. 'I am somewhat detained, but it's not a real drama,' was the message the nabbed mediator managed to phone in to the press.

These dramatic events constituted only the final chapter in what had been a slow and steady slide for the company. Under the management of Moulinex founder, Jean Mantelet, the company failed to anticipate the economic slowdown of the early 1980s, and from 1985 onwards losses began to mount up. Another problem related to the company's core product offering – microwave ovens. Asian manufacturers were flooding the European market with similar products, and often at lower prices. But still Moulinex continued to spend money, with a strategy based on the takeover of other companies, such as the luxury coffee-maker specialist Krups, which Moulinex acquired in 1987. Debts steadily grew, and in 1996 Moulinex tried to return to profit by laying off 2,600 workers. This tough measure worked, at least in the short term.

In 1997, the company declared a profit for the first time in years. However, the celebrations were short-lived. Not only had the job-cuts damaged the brand's reputation in France, the following year saw the new collapse of the Russian economy. As Russia was Moulinex's second largest market, sales were dramatically affected and the company went back into the red. Things got even worse with a similar economic crisis in Brazil, a country where Moulinex had made various acquisitions.

In September 2000, the company merged with the Italian company Brandt. This did nothing to prevent declining sales and rising debt. The bankruptcy filing in 2001 was a drastic, but almost inevitable last resort.

As Moulinex is still struggling to find a buyer, the omens are not good for one of France's most famous brands.

Lessons from Moulinex

- *Watch the competition*. Moulinex was caught off guard by the influx of microwaves from Asian manufacturers.
- *Watch the economy.* When economies are in trouble, so are brands. Following the economic crisis in Russia, Moulinex lost a major part of its market overnight.
- *Keep employers on side.* The numerous disputes did more to damage Moulinex's reputation in its native France than anything else.

96 *Nova* magazine

Let sleeping brands lie

In the 1960s *Nova* magazine was Britain's 'style bible', and had a massive impact on the fashion of the era. Alongside the fashion pages, it carried serious and often controversial articles on subjects such as feminism, homosexuality and racism. At the time, the magazine was unique, but by the 1970s other magazines started to clone the *Nova* concept. *Nova* itself soon started to look tired and fell victim to sluggish sales, and closed in 1975 after 10 years in operation – a lifetime in the magazine industry.

However, such was the impact of the magazine on its generation that IPC Magazines (which owns *Marie Claire* magazine) decided to relaunch the title in 2000. Second time around, the magazine was positioned as a lifestyle magazine that was as edgy and fashion-conscious as the original.

The first issue lived up to this promise. Here was a women's magazine completely devoid of articles such as '10 steps to improving your relationship', 'How to catch the perfect man' and 'Celebrities and their star-signs'. According to the *Guardian*, the revamped *Nova* 'had more humour than the failed *Frank* magazine, and more realistic fashion than *Vogue* while still being a clothes fantasy.'

Three months later though the publishers were already starting to worry that the sales figures were lower than they had anticipated. They therefore moved editor Deborah Bee, and replaced her with Jeremy Langmead, who had previously been the editor of the *Independent* newspaper's *Style* magazine. Although some commentators questioned the decision to place a man at the helm of a magazine aimed at women, gender wasn't the real problem. After all, *Elle* magazine had a male editor for many years without disastrous consequences.

Tim Brooks, the managing director of IPC, declared that the first three issues of *Nova* had been 'too edgy'. But the publishers had done little to calm wary consumers by shrink-wrapping the magazine in plastic. After all, most people who purchase a new, unfamiliar magazine want to flick through it first to check that the content is relevant to them.

The new editor was quick to make changes. The novelist, India Knight, was given her own column, and more mainstream features, such as an exercise page, soon appeared. Although the magazine gathered a loyal readership, the numbers weren't enough.

In May 2001, a year after its launch, IPC pulled the plug on *Nova*. 'It is with great reluctance that we have had to make this decision,' Tim Brooks said at the time. '*Nova* was ground-breaking in its style and delivery, but commercially has not reached its targets. IPC has an aggressive launch strategy, and an important part of this strategy is the strength to take decisive action and close unviable titles.' IPC also said that it wanted to concentrate on the bigger-selling *Marie Claire*.

For many, the failure of *Nova*'s second attempt was not a surprise. 'It was exactly like all the other magazines and failed to capture the British public's imagination,' said Caroline Baker, the fashion director at *You* magazine, and a journalist on the original *Nova*. 'They should have left the old one alone, not tried to bring it back.'

Whereas the original *Nova* had little competition when it launched, the updated version had entered a saturated market place. 2000 had seen a whole batch of new women's magazines enter the British market such as the pocket-sized and hugely successful *Glamour* magazine (the first edition sold 500,000 copies). Unlike *Nova*, *Glamour* had spent masses on making sure the magazine was moulded around the market. 'We travelled up and down the country and spoke to thousands of young women to ensure not just the right editorial, but the scale and size of the magazine,' said Simon Kippin, *Glamour*'s publisher.

The *Guardian* reported on the highly competitive nature of the women's magazine market where new titles are launched and extinguished with increasing speed:

The cycle of launches and closures may have speeded up but then so has society. Forty-four percent of revenue is currently generated by magazines that did not exist 10 years ago. People still like magazines, in fact 84 percent still believe that magazines are worth spending money on, according to Henley Centre research. The magazines that people enjoy buying however, are not guaranteed to remain the same.

Commentating on *Nova* and other magazine closures, Nicholas Coleridge, managing director of Conde Nast Publications, said magazine closures are a fact of life for the industry. 'It is not surprising nor horrific when magazines open and close,' he said. 'It's completely predictable, and it's been that way for hundreds of years, otherwise we would still be reading cave-man magazines.'

According to this logic the failure of *Nova* version two can be attributed to the natural order of magazine publishing. However, many have said that if *Nova* had been given more time to carve its niche, it would still be here today.

One thing though, seems certain. Having already been given a second chance, it is unlikely to be allowed a third. But then again. . .

Lessons from *Nova*

- *Recognize that brands have their time.* Just because *Nova* worked in the 1960s didn't mean that the same formula would still be relevant in the 21st century.
- *Account for brand failures.* Magazine publishers take a pragmatic approach to failure. Indeed, most factor in a couple of annual 'misses' into their budgets. 'Of every six magazines launched, two will fail,' says Conde Nast's Nicholas Coleridge.

97 Levi's

Below the comfort zone

Levi's is, without doubt, a classic brand. Originally produced by a Bavarian immigrant in the dying years of the battle for the American West, Levi's jeans now have an iconic significance across the globe.

Indeed, in many ways Levi's have come to define the very essence of the word 'brand' better than any other product. As advertising journalist Bob Garfield has written 'in literal terms, it's damn near the only true brand out there, burned into a thong of leather and stitched to the waistband.'

In its September 2002 edition, the UK version of *Esquire* magazine heralded Levi's as the ultimate clothing brand and a staple to the worldwide wardrobe:

> The secret behind the enduring magic and success of Levi's has been its ability to symbolise both ubiquity and uniqueness simultaneously. No other brand has managed to become part of the system (part of the President's wardrobe, even) while retaining a defining element of rebellion, revolution and counter-culture. Levi's are both fashion and anti-fashion. Just try to name someone you know who doesn't own at least one pair.

However, despite its continued ubiquity the Levi's brand has had a rocky ride in recent times, having watched sales slip from US $7.9 billion in 1996 to US $4.3 billion in 2001.

As with most brand crises, the problems for Levi's have been numerous. To understand them fully, it is necessary to appreciate the company's branding strategy. Levi's CEO Robert Haas told *The Financial Times* in 1998 (ironically one of the most uncomfortable of years for the brand):

> We are in the comfort business. I don't just mean physical comfort. I mean we are providing psychological comfort – the feeling of security that, when you enter a room of strangers or even work colleagues, you are attired within the brand of acceptability. Although what a consumer defines as psychological comfort may vary from sub-segment to sub-segment.

The key phrase here is that last one, 'from sub-segment to sub-segment'. In its attempts to be sensitive to the various fluctuations of taste among the denim-wearing public, Levi's has diversified its brand by creating a wide range of jean styles. Most significantly, it has branched out beyond its traditional 'red label' jeans and introduced a new sub-brand called 'Silvertab'. The company has also produced a cheaper range of jeans with orange tags.

Furthermore, the advertising campaign used to promote the Silvertab range in 2001 was among the most hated in recent history. Ad Age called the campaign 'insulting' and claimed it 'lacked branding'. Similarly, in 2002 the ads to promote Levi's low-rise jeans achieved an equally negative reception among certain critics.

However, not all the problems have been of Levi's making. For instance, it could do little to curb the rise of designer jeans such as those produced by Calvin Klein, Diesel and Tommy Hilfiger. All Levi's could do in the face of such a competition was to try and preserve the integrity of its brand. Even here, the brand ran into difficulty.

In the UK, the start of the new millennium saw Levi's become engaged in a very public battle with Tesco's supermarket. Tesco's claimed that consumers were paying too much for their Levi's and the supermarket wanted to sell Levi's in its own stores with a narrower profit margin. Levi's refused to sell its premium jeans, such as 501s, via the supermarket, and went to court to stop imports from outside Europe.

'Our brand is our most important asset,' explained Joe Middleton, Levi's European president. 'It's more valuable than all the other assets on our balance sheet. It's more valuable than our factories, our buildings, our warehouses and our inventory. We must have the right to control the destiny of that brand.'

Even the UK government joined in, attempting to persuade the European Union to allow supermarkets like Tesco's to import goods from anywhere in the world. However, Levi's insisted that Tesco's was missing the point, confusing the cost of making the jeans with the cost of marketing them. 'The important point,' said Middleton, 'is that all these costs are an investment in the brand. The true cost of making this jean is not just the factory element. It's much more than that.' The UK government, keen to eradicate the image of 'Rip-off Britain' has remained on the supermarket's side, and it looks like Levi's will eventually lose the battle.

Despite all these unfortunate external factors, there is no escaping the fact that the real threat to the Levi's brand is generated from Levi's itself. Now that it is locked in an endless quest to appear 'innovative' and 'youthful', by launching a growing number of new styles, Levi's is now proving the law of diminishing returns. The marketing expense continues to grow, while the true brand value diminishes.

The view within the business world has been articulated by Kurt Barnard, publisher of Barnard's *Retail Trend Report*, in *The Financial Times* in 2001. 'Levi's is basically a troubled company,' he said. 'Although their name is hallowed in American history, few people these days wear Levi's jeans.'

In 2000, the company failed to make the top 75 global brands by value according to the Interbrand 2000 Brand Valuation Survey. The inclusion of rival brands such as Gap and Benetton only served to rub more salt in Levi's wounds.

So what is the solution? Most branding experts now agree that if Levi's is going to regain the market position it held in the 1980s and early 1990s it will need to slim down and narrow its focus. Consumers are no longer sure what the Levi's brand stands for. Denim, yes. But what type? Straight-cut, loose fit, low rise, twisted, classic, contemporary. You name it, Levi's covers it.

It therefore needs to cure itself of what could reasonably be called 'Miller syndrome'. Just as Miller decided to be all beers to all people, Levi's is doing the same with jeans. But this does not mean that Levi's should stop launching new styles, just that it shouldn't do so under the Levi's name. Indeed, one of the company's biggest successes in recent times came when it created an entirely new identity in the form of the Dockers brand, launched in 1986.

For the Levi's brand itself, the solution, as with so many other troubled brands, may involve a recovery of its original values. Indeed, there are signs that this is already happening. In 2001, the company paid out US $46,532 for the oldest pair of the Levi's blue jeans in existence, named the Nevada Jeans, when they were advertised on eBay. A few months later the company launched a limited edition of 500 replicas, which were sold almost as soon as they appeared in special Levi's concept stores.

Only time will tell if this Vintage collection turns out to be a symbolic gesture of the brand's new direction.

Lessons from Levi's

- *Intensify, don't multiply.* Instead of accentuating its core brand values, Levi's has confused jeans buyers with an apparently limitless array of different styles. As brand expert Al Ries has put it: 'In the long term, expanding your brand will diminish your power and weaken your image.'
- *Focus on your strengths.* If Levi's stands for anything it stands for 'the original jean'. In order to fully recover it will need to consolidate and strengthen this identity.
- *Don't look down on your original brand.* When Levi's launched the Silvertab range it fell into the same trap as Coca-Cola when they launched New Coke. As branding expert and journalist Ian Cocoran has pointed out, 'Levi's now seems to have a real problem in convincing the consumer that ownership of the previously indomitable red label still represents sufficient kudos to command exclusivity.'

98 Kmart

A brand on the brink

One of the United States' largest chain of discount stores, Kmart filed for bankruptcy on 22 January 2002. The action came after poor Christmas sales and the company's inability to pay its major suppliers.

The bankruptcy filing was viewed by the US business media as the culmination of a series of mistakes under Kmart's CEO Chuck Conaway, who took over in May 2000 and launched a US $2 billion overhaul to clean up dingy stores and improve the company's outdated distribution systems. These distribution flaws had led to many of Kmart's most publicized ranges not being found by customers. For instance, when Martha Stewart launched her 'Keeping' line of brand merchandise exclusively for Kmart in June 2000 she had to tell customers: 'If you're frustrated, keep looking.'

While facing an uphill battle with distribution, Conaway embarked on a price war, challenging rival stores Wal-Mart and Target on price. The tactic failed. Wal-Mart fought back even more aggressively, Target sued, and Kmart sales remained disappointingly stagnant.

Conaway was also criticized for drastically cutting Kmart's advertising spend. Analysts believe he should have used advertising to tell consumers about the expensive clean-up operation. Kurt Barnard, publisher of Barnard's *Retail Trend Report* said:

> I was very apprehensive when Chuck inherited Kmart and its creaky operations. But he did the right thing by diverting hundreds of millions

to the stores in cleaning them up. Trouble was, he failed to let 270 million shoppers know that Kmart is a new store for the American family. Meanwhile, 270 million American shoppers kept nursing the image that Kmart was a dirty place and had too much stock.

Whether or not Kmart will be able to recover from bankruptcy and take on its stronger-than-ever rivals remains to be seen.

Lessons from Kmart

- *Realize that price gimmicks won't win long-term customers.* 'The problem was that Wal-Mart and Target were out there pitching low prices, broad inventories, hip products, and pleasant shopping experiences while Kmart was banking everything on random in-store discounts,' reported *Business 2.0* magazine. Kmart needed to communicate a reason for consumers to shop there – and shop often.
- *Don't neglect advertising.* A retailer undergoing a great deal of change needs to tell the public about it on a regular basis. Instead, Kmart cut its newspaper advertising.
- *Be better than the competition.* This is a tough challenge. Wal-Mart is a retailing giant, while Target has been called 'quite possibly the best run company in the world,' in Sam Hill's book on branding, *The Infinite Asset.*

99 The Cream nightclub

Last dance saloon?

In the 1990s Liverpool nightclub Cream grew from being a small intimate venue catering for around 400 clubbers every Saturday night, to being one of the UK's first 'super clubs' regularly attracting thousands of devotees from all over the country. It quickly capitalized on its success by launching merchandising material, setting up its own record label in partnership with Virgin, touring nationally and internationally with a variety of sponsors, and even embarking on a series of dance music festivals called Creamfields, catering for around 40,000 clubbers. By the end of the 1990s there were regular Cream nights in places as far afield as Buenos Aires and Ibiza, as well as the brand's native Liverpool.

Yet in September 2002, Cream co-founder and boss James Barton announced that the Liverpool club was closing. Although Barton said the reason for the closure was to concentrate on other aspects of the company, he also admitted to Radio One that 'if the club was doing the sort of numbers it was doing four or five years ago we wouldn't be making this decision.' The media responded by saying that the decision not only signified the imminent death of the Cream brand, but of club culture in general. Whether or not Cream manages to survive without its spiritual home remains to be seen, but the closure certainly indicates tough times ahead.

So why exactly did it happen? How could a club that became a household name for a generation suddenly lose its appeal? The reasons, as you might well expect, are numerous.

One argument was that as Cream expanded it gradually lost its cool factor. In 1992, the year James Barton and Darren Hughes set up the club, Cream was immediately viewed as a welcome antidote to the business-minded approach of the London club, Ministry of Sound.

Word of mouth helped to fuel its early growth, along with celebratory pieces in dance music magazines such as *Mixmag* which named Cream its 'club of the year' in 1994. Around this time Cream decided to expand its operation, moving the club to a larger venue and launching nights in Ibiza. By the middle of the decade, Cream was everywhere. Clubbers were sporting tattoos of the distinctive Cream logo (which itself had won awards for its 'propeller-style' design), DJs from around the world were lining up to play in the main room, and one Liverpool couple even decided to get married at a Cream event. In 1996, Cream was cited as the third main reason people applied to Liverpool University in a poll conducted by the university. Over 60,000 people rushed out to buy the 'Cream Live' CD in the first week of release.

Then, in 1998, the first signs of trouble started to appear. Darren Hughes left the company to set up his own super club, Home, in London's Leicester Square. The year after the first 'Creamfields' festival, Hughes started his own 'Homelands' event. The club's former director was now the competition.

Another problem was the cost of putting on Cream events at the Liverpool club. Ironically, for a club which helped to establish the cult of the 'superstar DJ', the fees charged by big names such as Fatboy Slim, Sasha, Paul Oakenfold, the Chemical Brothers and Carl Cox were becoming the major weekly cost. However, without paying for the DJs, Cream would have risked losing its market altogether. 'It's the performers who make the real money, though they used to draw in enough custom to make it worth the club's while,' says *Mixmag* editor Viv Craske. 'Big clubs still rely on the same old DJs, despite no longer drawing the crowds.' With big names typically charging four or five figure sums for two hours' work, the costs could clearly be crippling for a club such as Cream which always advertised their events on the strength of their DJ line-ups.

Another factor, and one beyond Cream's immediate control, was the fact that its original customer was now getting too old to be on the dance floor at three in the morning every Saturday night. For many 18-year-olds, the idea of 'super clubs' and 'superstar DJs' was starting to be wholly unattractive. As Jacques Peretti wrote in a July 2002 article in the *Guardian*, this generational shift took place at the end of the 1990s:

These teenagers were more interested in rebelling against their siblings and joining a band. Instead of going to clubs, it became cool to follow American nu-metal bands such as Slipknot and Papa Roach – bands that preach hate and pain in ludicrous gothic garb, not peace and love, as ageing house DJs might. [. . .] Even to their natural constituency, super clubs epitomised everything that had gone wrong with club culture [. . .] The cutting edge of this culture now is not Cream or Ministry of Sound, but tiny venues with a word-of-mouth following.

As Cream became ever-more commercial, it was seen to lose its point. What did it have to offer which couldn't be provided by mass-market pub, club and restaurant corporations such as Luminar and First Leisure (which began to borrow the super clubs' music policy for their own venues but without having to fork out for the high profile DJ)? Cream, and the other super clubs, had suddenly seemed to lose their sense of creativity and personality. (It is perhaps not a coincidence that in 2002, the year Cream shut its Liverpool club, the biggest nightclub event in the UK was School Disco – which completely rejected the dance music ethos in favour of unpretentious good fun, with clubbers dressing in school uniforms and dancing to Duran Duran and Dexy's Midnight Runners).

Some people have also questioned the competence of Cream's management team. The owners certainly had no formal training, as with most people in the clubbing industry. As Oxford graduate, former merchant banker, chairman and co-founder of Ministry of Sound, James Palumbo, once put it: 'The world of nightclubs is so populated by incompetent people that you only have to be a bit better to make a success of it.'

This accusation is at least partly unfair though. In many ways Cream has been too 'business-like', at least ostentatiously. In an interview with the *Liverpool Echo*, James Barton was asked about the decision to close the club. 'It is something which is unfortunate but I think we have to make these sorts of decisions,' he said. 'At the end of the day we are businessmen.' Of course, they *are* businessmen, but that doesn't mean they have to advertise the fact. Equally, they were perhaps unwise to make such a big deal out of their tenth anniversary.

Cream is, or at least should be, a youth brand. As such it needs to be about the here and now, not the past. As one anonymous commentator remarked on the Internet, 'when was the last time you watched other youth brands like Nike or Nintendo celebrate their birthdays.' Certainly, when your core market is 18–24 year-olds the last thing you want to be telling them is that you are 10 years old. They don't care about what you were doing when they were, in some cases, only eight years old.

The club's reputation has also been tarnished by its association with drug use. Merseyside Police expressed concerns in 2000 about the 'drug culture' at Cream, saying it could have taken more measures to prevent drug dealing at the venue. In 1999, a 21-year-old woman died after collapsing on the dance floor.

Although James Barton said after the club's closure that the German brand remains at 'the forefront of youth culture' there is an increasing amount of evidence to the contrary. Its 'Cream Collect' album sold under 2,000 copies in total.

Competitors have also been quick to isolate themselves from the Cream closure, by blaming a lack of brand innovation. 'Cream closing is a seminal moment in club land history,' Ministry of Sound managing director Mark Rodol told the *Independent* newspaper. 'It's a lesson to club promoters that you can't sit still. Ministry of Sound's music policy changes at least every twelve months and has always done so, with our nights proving there's still thousands of clubbers looking for a great night out.'

Although it remains to be seen whether the Cream brand will turn sour, or once again be able to rise to the top, there is no denying it needs a radical overhaul if it is to survive. 'Clubs like Cream no longer empathise with customers,' says *Mixmag*'s Crastke. 'They've lost the trust of the kids. And once you've lost the kids, it's very hard to get them back.'

Lessons from Cream

- *Don't contradict your brand values.* If you're a nightclub which is open until six in the morning, your key market tends to be people under 24 years old. It was a mistake then to emphasize the age and longevity of the Cream brand to a market which cares little about such values.
- *Adapt or die.* For youth brands, the only constant is change. The Cream nightclub relied on the same tried and tested formula for too long, using expensive DJs who had passed their sell-by date.
- *Avoid over-exposure.* By 2000, Cream could be found everywhere. At festivals, in clothes shops, in music stores, on TV adverts. As the brand extended its line however, the identity became diluted and consequently the club struggled to attract enough custom to keep it going.

- *Watch market trends.* The fact that 200,000 people went to see Fatboy Slim live on Brighton beach in the same month that Cream closed down proved that there was still a strong market for dance music events. It also proved that the Cream nightclub may have been moving in the wrong direction.

100 Yardley cosmetics

From grannies to handcuffs

How does a once supremely successful brand descend into failure? The answer, in the case of Yardley cosmetics, is by failing to move with the times.

Yardley was founded in London in 1770 by William Yardley, a purveyor of swords, spurs and buckles for the aristocracy. He took over a lavender soap business from his son-in-law William Cleaver who had gambled away his inheritance. Throughout the next 200 years the brand grew from strength to strength with its portfolio of flower-scented soaps, talcum powders and traditional perfumes.

Yardley's brand identity was quintessentially English, and it supplied soaps and perfumes to the Queen and the Queen Mother. However, during the 1960s Yardley was seen as a cool brand associated with swinging London. 'The English Rose image was a digression,' said Yardley's former chief executive Richard Finn. 'In the 1960s, Yardley was associated with Twiggy, Carnaby Street and mini skirts, not stuck in a cottage garden with green wellies.'

The following decades saw the brand slide back towards a conservative image, as the age of the average customer grew older. By the start of the 1990s its 'granny image' was being commented on by certain British journalists. When SmithKline Beecham bought the company in 1990 for £110 million, it embarked on numerous attempts to spruce up the brand's identity.

In 1997, the company changed its advertising model from actress Helena Bonham Carter to supermodel Linda Evangelista. One of the adverts showed her shackled in chains and handcuffs – a long way from grannies and green wellies. But the multi-million pound advertising campaign failed to work. In fact, it served only to alienate the brand's most loyal customers.

On 26 August 1998 the company went into receivership with debts of about £120 million. The brand eventually found a buyer in the form of German hair care giant Wella. It remains to be seen whether Wella will be able to modernize the Yardley brand.

Lessons from Yardley

- *Don't neglect your core customers.* Brands must try to change over time without neglecting their traditional customers.
- *Remember that historical brands carry historical baggage.* The Yardley brand identity had evolved over more than two hundred years. It couldn't be erased with one advertising campaign.

References

Barger, S (2000) *Hell's Angel: The life and times of Sonny Barger and the Hell's Angels Motorcycle Club*, William Morrow and Co, New York

Cassel, J and Jenkins, H (1998) *From Barbie to Mortal Kombat: Gender and computer games*, MIT Press, Cambridge MA

Cassidy, J (2002) *Dot.con: The greatest story ever sold*, HarperCollins, New York

Cellan-Jones, R (2001) *Dot.bomb: The rise and fall of dot.com Britain*, Aurum Press, London

Dearlove, D and Crainer, S (1999) *The Ultimate Book of Business Brands: Insights from the world's 50 greatest brands*, Capstone Publishing Limited, Dover, NH

Enrico, R (1986) *The Other Guy Blinked: How Pepsi won the cola wars*, Bantam Books, New York

Garrett, L (1994) *The Coming Plague: Newly emerging diseases in a world out of balance*, Farrar, Straus and Giroux, New York

Haig, M (2002) *Mobile Marketing: the marketing revolution*, Kogan Page, London

Hill, S, Lederer, C and Lane Keller, K (2001) *The Infinite Asset: Managing brands to build new value*, Harvard Business School Press, Boston, MA

Iacocca, L (1986) *Iacocca: An autobiography*, Bantam Books, New York

Janal, D (2001) *Branding the Net*, http://brandingthenet.com

Klein, N (2000) *No Logo: Taking aim at the brand bullies*, Picador, New York

Lacey, R (1988) *Ford: The men and the machine*, Little, Brown and Company, Boston, MA and Toronto

Lardner, J (1987) *Fast Forward: Hollywood, the Japanese, and the onslaught of the VCR*, WW Norton & Company, New York

Malmsten, E, Portanger, E and Drazin, C (2001) *Boo Hoo: A dot com story*, Random House Business Books, London

McMath, R (1999) *What Were They Thinking?*, Times Books, New York

Mello, S (2001) *Customer Centric Product Definition: The key to great product development*, AMACOM, New York

Murphy, P (1991) Game theory models for organizational/public conflict, *Canadian Journal of Communication*, **16** (2)

Ottman, J (1998) *Green Marketing: Opportunities for innovation in the new marketing age*, Ntc Business Books, Lincolnwood, IL

Peters, T (1997) *The Circle of Innovation*, Alfred A Knopf, New York

Ries, A and Ries, L (1998) *The 22 Immutable Laws of Branding*, Harper Collins Business, New York

Ries, A and Trout, J (1993) *The 22 Immutable Laws of Marketing: Violate them at your own risk*, Harper Collins Business, New York

Searles, D, Locke, C, Levine, R and Weinberger, D (2001) *The Cluetrain Manifesto: The end of business as usual*, Perseus Publishing, Cambridge, MA

Trout, J (2001) *Big Brands, Big Trouble: Lessons learned the hard way*, John Wiley & Sons, New York

Trout, J (2000) *Differentiate or Die: Survival in our era of killer competition*, John Wiley & Sons, New York

Trout, J (1995) *The New Positioning: The latest on the world's number one business strategy*, McGraw-Hill Trade, New York

Vidal, J (1997) *McLibel: Burger culture on trial*, Macmillan, London

Wolf, M J (1999) *The Entertainment Economy: How mega-media forces are transforming our lives*, Times Books, New York

Index